Berkeley One and Only

Jon Sullivan
with Contee Seely

Edited by
Contee Seely and Daphne O'Neal

Command Performance Press
Berkeley

Orders, inquiries and correspondence should be directed to:

Command Performance Press
1755 Hopkins Street
Berkeley, CA 94707
Tel/Fax 510-524-1191
www.berkeleyoneandonly.com

Printed in China
on acid-free paper.

First edition

ISBN-13: 978-0-929724-52-2
ISBN-10: 0-929724-52-6

Library of Congress Control Number: 2005934764

Dedication

Dedicated to the Huchiun of the Ohlone people, who lived for hundreds of generations on the land that would become Berkeley. To José Domingo Peralta, the first European resident and owner of the land, who lost it all in the labyrinth of California law. To 49er Captain James Jacobs and those who followed him to the village of Ocean View. To the early farmers whose enterprise is now marked by street names: Ashby, Curtis, Kelsey, McGee, Webster and Woolsey. To the trustees of the College of California who brought their institution to the forks of Strawberry Creek. To Phoebe Apperson Hearst, who adopted the university and promoted its growth. To protester Mary Henderson, who twice moved her house on top of the Central Pacific Railroad tracks. To August Vollmer, the first police chief, who brought the city innovative community policing. To capitalist Francis Marion "Borax" Smith, whose combination of electric rail lines and land development spawned a superb interurban rail system. To the flamboyant character and wildly successful actor Maurice B. Curtis, whose blazing career was extinguished by a tragic legal entanglement. To Bernard Maybeck, whose inspired architecture changed the face and philosophy of Berkeley. To Mario Savio, whose "operation of the machine" speech became one of the city's fundamental documents. To our partners, Maggie Seely and Joann Sullivan, whose gracious support made this project possible. And to Christina and Michael Seely and Jessica, Margaret and Nicholas Sullivan, who brought joy and hard work to the project.

Sunrise at Inspiration Point in Tilden Park
paints the landscape. As layers of fog separate and
congeal in the intensifying light, the rich colors rapidly change and then disappear.

Table of Contents

Moments after sunrise, the hills begin to glow a golden brown and the fog thins and darkens. The landscape emerges from darkness and fog and becomes quintessentially Californian.

Foreword

We love Berkeley. If we attempted to create a single image to display all its wonders, what would it look like? Hour by hour everything would be shifting — colors, composition, skin tones, feelings, weather. We would revel in a breathtaking kaleidoscope, continually surprising. The photos in *Berkeley One and Only* are but fragmentary glimpses of life in this extraordinary town.

Not everything about Berkeley is perceptible from the images here. We generally share a range of unphotographable "progressive" attitudes and beliefs relating to war, the environment, abortion, government policies, corporations, science, civil rights, affirmative action and more.

Berkeley still is widely regarded as the seat of liberal and radical ferment in the U.S. but is far calmer than it was in the '60s when Vietnam War protests, the invasion by the National Guard and the Free Speech Movement occurred.

Certainly the city would not be what it is without the university, which infuses Berkeley life with a stimulating array of the intellectual, the artistic, the practical. The student body itself is a significant determinant in the character of the town. For most of the university's history, it was predominantly white. Now it is about a third white and a third Asian and Asian-American.

We love the variety of flora, the hills, the bay, the views, the benign year-round weather and tantalizing nearby locales (such as San Francisco, Napa Valley, Monterey and Yosemite). The contentiousness of city politics, the active cultural and intellectual life and the ethnic and racial mix (about 59% white, 16% Asian, 14% black, 10% Hispanic and 5% others) enhance our lives. Fresh and organic foods, neighborhood specialty shops and a remarkable diversity of restaurants contribute to the exceptional panorama that is Berkeley.

How did we Berkeleyites get here? Some were born here and never left. Some came to study or to visit and found they could not leave. Some came to check out this famously unique town and deemed it at least as desirable a place to live as any. And some can't bear the thought of living anywhere else. A neighbor once told me, as he waved eastward, "It's dangerous beyond those hills."

Contee Seely
September, 2006

Kites fill the air at the Berkeley Kite Festival in
César Chávez Park. The steady marine breeze
through the Golden Gate makes the waterfront
park one of the nation's best kite-flying venues.

Introduction

All photographs are historical documents. Society, technology and the natural world are all changing so rapidly that every picture is bounded in time. From the beginning Berkeley has been a center of industrial, social and intellectual ferment. There are no pictures of timeless Berkeley. Despite an active and forceful preservationist movement, change is everywhere.

Fifteen years ago Contee dreamed of a book of color photographs of Berkeley as a way of bringing to print images of our common experience of living in Berkeley. On the most prosaic of errands — visiting the dentist, grocery shopping — we would casually look up and catch our breath at the city's beauty. Berkeley is in a stunning natural setting and permeated by active artistic and intellectual spirits. We are a town of free thinkers bubbling with creativity and change.

Amidst busy lives and full-time jobs, we began taking photographs in 1997. Except for an occasional retake, photography ended in 2003. The first realization of the dream was a very large-format book with a catalog of small images. Over time we decided to let the city come to life through fewer and larger photographs. We looked at numerous books for inspiration, but Galen Rowell's impressive *Bay Area Wild* set the best example with its simple design and fine photography.

As the work progressed, we realized that a city as storied as Berkeley needed more text to bring the images to life. There is a considerable amount of history in the essays that begin each chapter and in commentary that accompanies the pictures. *Berkeley One and Only* is also peppered with current facts, natural history and social commentary.

We focused on compelling images from over 6,000 photographs. Our method was to let the pictures determine the book's themes and chapters. A few striking photographs are placed between the chapters and at the beginning and end of the book.

Although we reached out to find special images of Berkeley, the final product is inevitably a reflection of our beginning. This is a book about hometown Berkeley.

The Berkeley pier was originally built far out into the
shallow bay as the terminus for the San Francisco ferry.
The distant Berkeley hills and the nearby marina are under
a cloudy winter sky.

Strolling under a deciduous magnolia in full
bloom are a woman with baby carriage and dog.
Even though February is one of Berkeley's coldest
months and the middle of the rainy season, many
plants are beginning to quicken and flower. By mid-
February or earlier, the city is filled with flowers.
On Lincoln Street ornamental plums planted by the
Works Progress Administration are covered with
clouds of pink blossoms. Magnolia cultivars, fruiting plums and acacia trees are in bloom. There are
bearded irises, daffodils, flowering quince and nar-
cissus. The small shrub *Daphne odora* broadcasts its
intoxicating perfume.

2

About Town

A thousand flowers bloom in Berkeley. Here plants from all climates thrive, as does a bewildering swirl of ideas and cultures. Its grand University of California is a global garden of exquisite intellect. Many outsiders think of the city as homogeneous, but precisely the opposite is true. Beautiful, passionate Berkeley revels in the ecstatic blossoming of art, architecture, books, controversy, cuisine, education, gardens, history, ideas, individuality, music, neighborhoods, parks, politics, science, sports, technology and theater. There is no impetus towards social conformity. Everyone follows their passion. Everyone is engaged. It is a constant surprise and delight to wander though the city's exotica.

The trustees of the College of California, the university's predecessor, were attracted by the unsurpassed natural beauty of a location between the branches of Strawberry Creek. It lay directly opposite the Golden Gate with sweeping vistas of the shimmering Bay and the distant coastal hills. The site's Mediterranean climate made it irresistible. Beautiful spring-like days of warm sunshine, caressing breezes and brilliant skies occur every month of the year. The cool California Current sweeping south along the coast modulates the climate. A cleansing ocean breeze flows through the Golden Gate and washes over the city.

Throughout its history the city's felicitous climate and the university's intellectual ferment have attracted characters, artists and activists. A number of sea captains retired in Berkeley, including Orrin Simmons, who sold the first parcel of land to the College of California. The exuberantly successful actor Maurice B. Curtis became a flamboyant capitalist and creator of the improbably elaborate Peralta Park Hotel (1888). The first activist, Mrs. Mary Henderson, twice moved her house directly onto the Shattuck Avenue railroad tracks in 1896 to protest the city's encroachments on her property. A swelling number of writers, beginning with Lincoln Steffens and Frank Norris, have made Berkeley their home and subject.

The tradition of Berkeley's early characters continues today. The mastery of science, technology and art of the early sea captains is brought into the 21st century by the scientists of Lawrence Berkeley Laboratory. Perhaps no one will ever match the flamboyance of M.B. Curtis, but the How Berkeley Can You Be? Parade is a grand display of showmanship and eccentricity. In the tradition of Mrs. Henderson, all varieties of social protest are an integral part of community life. Although the mass of Berkeley is staunchly progressive, a city council meeting or a walk through Sproul Plaza will reveal passionate support for conservative and Christian causes. There are about 200 places of worship, some of which are architectural triumphs.

From its beginnings in Ocean View and the College community, Berkeley grew slowly until the population boom that followed the 1906 San Francisco earthquake. By the 1930s buildings in a host of architectural styles occupied almost all of the available land. Most of these still survive despite a rash of boxy apartment buildings in the 1950s and '60s. As its heritage began to disappear, the city enacted the Neighborhood Preservation Ordinance (1973), followed later by protection for commercial buildings. A stroll through the city is a tour of its history. There are no big box stores and very few franchises. Berkeley is a city of small select shops and excellent independent restaurants. In recent years there has been steady development in its commercial corridors, but the city looks much as it did in the 1940s.

Saturday travelers board a southbound train at the Ashby BART station. Patrons give the service high marks. It is by far the Bay Area's fastest method of travel. Each weekday about 18,000 people arrive in Berkeley on BART. Trains arrive and depart every 15 or 20 minutes. Commuters dream of the day when BART will circle the bay and freeway congestion will be ameliorated.

The system is completely below ground in Berkeley with the exception of a few blocks near the city limits. In the original plan the tracks would only have been buried beneath Shattuck between Dwight Way and Hearst Street. The city revolted at this noisy, unsightly intrusion and supplied the necessary funds to build the tracks and stations underground.

From Alcatraz Avenue to downtown, BART follows the path of the Central Pacific steam train that first brought mass transit to Berkeley in 1876.

For 30 years Joseph Charles waved to the morning traffic on Martin Luther King Jr. Way calling out, "Have a GOOD day." He became a local and then a national and international legend. His irrepressible good humor warmed people's hearts and gave generations of children lasting memories. After retiring in 1992, he received many honors from the city. The community mourned his passing at 92 in 2002. In his final years he could be briefly persuaded to resume his post. Motorists honked and waved as if he had never left.

Above Tables heaped with farm-fresh produce and vendor-produced foods greet visitors at the busy Berkeley Farmer's Market. People chat with neighbors and fill cloth bags with all manner of locally grown produce.

Happy Boy Farms has a complex operation in the Monterey Bay area comprising six farms in different microclimates. They specialize in certified organic produce marketed directly to stores, restaurants and the general public.

Below Berkeley has a long-term homeless population estimated at between 800 and 1000 people. The city draws them because of its many social services and progressive attitudes. Although it is roundly criticized along with all authority, Berkeley's active and community-centered police force provides a measure of personal safety lacking elsewhere.

Left The city's hillside streets usually follow circuitous routes along the land's natural contours. Early developers provided a network of pedestrian paths to the city's network of rail lines. Today the rustic trails are one of the city's treasures.

Right The newly restored Marin Circle fountain in its Christmas finery. In 1958 a roofing truck plunged down Marin Avenue, the city's steepest street, and destroyed the original 1911 fountain.

The Greenwood Common complex (1952) features low-roofed houses in earth tones clustered around a central open green. The park-like development integrates architecture into landscape design. The style is known as the Second Bay Tradition (the First being exemplified by the work of Bernard Maybeck and Julia Morgan).

Above Alcatraz Island is perfectly framed by the street of the same name. Now part of the Golden Gate National Recreation Area, the island is a popular tourist destination. The storied island was long the site of a notorious federal prison and later subject to occupation by the American Indian Movement.

Below Shattuck Avenue on a peaceful Sunday. The avenue is wide enough for a median strip, four lanes of traffic and protected pull-in parking, because it once accommodated tracks for steam trains and electric trolleys. Every few minutes trains still run along Shattuck, but below ground.

On Sunday morning Berkeley becomes a small mid-American city. The Asamblea de Dios, or Templo Getsemani, is an eclectic Christian church with bilingual services in Spanish and English. In Berkeley services are held in a great variety of languages.

The Church of the Good Shepherd (1878) and the First Presbyterian Church (1879), Berkeley's first churches, are a few blocks away from the Asamblea de Dios. Churchmen founded the College of California, and today's Graduate Theological Union, comprised of nine seminaries, borders the university.

The Congregation Beth Israel is Berkeley's oldest and largest orthodox synagogue. For years there was a community garden next to the building. The charming brick structure above was demolished in 2004. The new larger building retains some of the original's architectural motifs.

Christian and Jewish traditions are very strong, but there is a wide variety of other religions. The city boasts nine Buddhist temples or centers representing various traditions. Lower University Avenue has a strong Hindu presence. New Age spiritual groups abound.

St. John's Presbyterian Church (1908-1910) is Julia Morgan's most accomplished wooden structure. The structural grace and patterning of the interior crossbeams and posts make the sanctuary warm and intimate. Exposed redwood is used throughout. Morgan built the large church for very little money; redwood was an inexpensive, native material.

A threat to the structure in 1971 awakened the neighborhood preservation movement that later affected all of Berkeley. The church is now the protean Julia Morgan Center for the Performing Arts.

Bernard Maybeck's First Church of Christ, Scientist (1910), masterfully uses light, color, Gothic tracery, exposed timbering and elaborate detail to create an awe-inspiring reverential experience. He combines Gothic, Byzantine, Romanesque and Japanese elements with modern material such as cast concrete, redwood timbering and asbestos paneling. It is Berkeley's first National Landmark.

The Berkeley High School Community Theater
(1950) was a WPA project delayed by the war. Incor-
porated into the lower part of the Art Deco building
is the Florence Schwimley Little Theater (1907). The
striking bas-relief mural has two trumpeting her-
alds and figures representing sculpture, painting,
music, dance, poetry and drama. It is by Robert
Howard, son of architect John Galen Howard.

14

Like many of the city's early architects, John Bakewell and Arthur Brown Jr. studied at Paris' École des Beaux-Arts. They modeled Berkeley's original City Hall (1910) on the town hall in Tours, France, designed by one of Brown's professors. Their firm also designed San Francisco City Hall with a nearly identical cupola. The building is now home of the Berkeley Unified School District.

Legendary councilwoman, Maudelle Shirek,
thoughtfully considers matters amid the tumult of a
city council meeting. The energetic Shirek began
her 20-year service on the council at the age of 74.
An unflagging progressive activist, she has been
honored and arrested many times. Berkeley named
the 1910 City Hall for her, after Congress refused
Representative Barbara Lee's request to so grace the
main Post Office.

Above The city council is a decorous body, but its meetings are a study in passionate, often unwieldy citizen participation. The audience frequently overflows the council chambers in the original City Hall. There is inspired partisan rhetoric, performance art and outrageous dress. The council occasionally promulgates its own foreign policy.

This 1998 council meeting debates an ordinance that would prohibit sitting on the street. Gatherings of street youth and dogs were angering merchants. Other audience members promote common decency, not an idle topic in Berkeley.

Below The X-plicit Players have been a thorn in the side of the city government for years. The city had an ordinance against pubic nudity, but Berkeley juries would not convict. The offence was demoted to a misdemeanor not subject to jury trial without noticeable effect. The group performs at the How Berkeley Can You Be? Parade and other events.

When the Pacifica Foundation took control of Berkeley's beloved KPFA in 1999, activists barricaded the thoroughfare in front of the station. The city rallied to the cry "KPFA is under attack." Protesters chained themselves to the station's doors. Tents sprouted up before the building. Ten thousand people marched through the streets. In Berkeley free speech is not negotiable. The activists prevailed.

The shock of September 11, 2001 brought
Berkeley residents into the streets. A traffic island at
Hopkins and Sonoma became a shrine for nightly
candlelight vigils. Three potted trees were set out
with lines strung between them. A circle of candles
was placed inside. Grieving citizens lighted candles
and hung heartfelt prayers. The memorial contin-
ued for many months in various forms.

On a beautiful summer day strollers wander by a couple relaxing on the steps of the elegant United States Post Office (1914). The building's graceful colonnade is reminiscent of Foundling Hospital in Florence, Italy, built during the Renaissance. Terra cotta embellishments with classical motifs line the high arches and create horizontal bands around the building. The façade's arches are repeated above the openings in the entrance wall and above the clerks' stations. At the west end of the lobby is a small WPA mural of early Berkeley settlers by Suzanne Scheuer.

When the College of California first opened in 1873, John G. Wright, the city's first baker, offered students room and board. His establishment on Shattuck Avenue prospered and became the Golden Sheaf Bakery a few years later. Wright was active in the union, temperance and women's suffrage movements. He helped feed the refugees after the great San Francisco earthquake.

Eventually the bakery became one of the city's largest employers. Unfortunately the day of large family-owned bakeries passed and the business was sold to Wonder Bread in 1909.

Wright constructed the handsome brick-faced Golden Sheaf Bakery Annex (1905) on Addison Street as a warehouse. For most of the century the building was used as commercial space and then a garage. In 2000 Avi Nevo renovated the building and donated it to the Berkeley Repertory Theater. The façade was restored with three open bays below the paired windows. Today the hundred-year-old terra cotta sheaf of wheat stands gracefully over the building and the Addison Street Arts District.

Kandy's Full Service Car Wash and Detail occupies a former gas station on Sacramento Street. It is one of a cluster of small businesses between Oregon and Alcatraz in the historic Lorin or South Berkeley district. The district was one of the few places where African-Americans migrating to the World War II shipyards could find decent housing.

In the background are units of the William Byron Rumford Sr. Plaza, named for a Sacramento Street pharmacist who became an influential state assemblyman. Rumford authored seminal fair employment and housing legislation.

On Addison Street, the side of the Heywood building (1906) features the faded advertisements from a bygone era. Next to it are the rounded bay windows and distinctive mansard roof of the Studio building (1905). The buildings are remnants of the past, when steam trains brought San Francisco commuters to Berkeley Station, which is now occupied by Shattuck Square (1926). Beyond are the tan bricks of the generic Kress building (1932).

The Addison Arts District with its Poetry Walk and Berkeley Repertory Theater are just to the west.

Alice Waters' Chez Panisse is a cornerstone of Berkeley's thriving food culture. It is California cuisine at its absolute best. It serves a single menu that changes each day to take advantage of the freshest possible ingredients from handpicked providers. Waters' culinary achievements have earned her worldwide recognition.

Across the street are the extraordinary breads and cheeses of the Cheese Board Collective. Its takeout pizza shop always has a long line winding down the street for the day's single offering.

Within the block are a host of gourmet offerings, each with its loyal following: coffee and tea at Peet's; Spanish tapas at César; Thai food at Cha Am; and French cuisine at diminutive Grégoire's. But this is only a taste of the many fine restaurants and shops along Shattuck Avenue and throughout the city.

Above Underneath Spenger's parking lot are the remains of a great shell mound built up over centuries by native Ohlone Indians. Late in the 1800s the site was converted into Willow Grove Park, a popular beer garden.

In 1890 Johann Spenger opened a grocery with a rudimentary bar and crab stand to serve the park. The establishment evolved into one of the nation's most successful restaurants. It prospered until 1998, when grandson Frank Spenger Jr. retired and the original restaurant closed. The photograph was taken just before the closing. Eventually, a corporation reopened the restaurant.

Below In 1903 an electric streetcar line stimulated growth at the intersection of College and Ashby. Elmwood Park, east of College, gave the district its name. The area boomed after the 1906 earthquake. Unique in Berkeley, the shopping district has the character of a small town center with a drugstore, bank, grocery, library, post office, shops and theater.

World War II veteran flyer Charles "Ozzie" Osborne bought the drugstore soda fountain and quickly made it a local favorite. Small town neighborliness flourished around him. When escalating rents threatened Ozzie's in 1981, the city passed a commercial rent control ordinance. The Elmwood Pharmacy became a symbol of Berkeley's determination to preserve its quality of life.

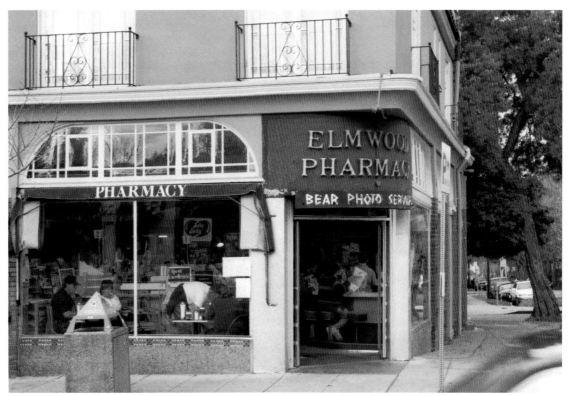

Above Berkeley Youth Alternatives (BYA) began as a runaway house on Telegraph Avenue at the height of the 1960s cultural revolution. BYA has changed with the times but always focused on at-risk youth. Gathering solid community support from diverse sources such as the Golden State Warriors, Sybase Corporation and UC Berkeley, the organization has prospered. It boasts a girl's basketball league, computer training and a commercial garden. Keeping pace with Berkeley's culinary revolution, BYA recently expanded to include a fully equipped commercial training kitchen.

Below At the end of a busy day, people descend into the downtown Berkeley BART station. From its 19th-century beginnings, Berkeley developed around interurban rail transportation.

Young children love to scramble through the giant DNA sculpture at the Lawrence Hall of Science. The combination of scientific exhibit and play structure invites the life force it illustrates.

The picture looks east over downtown Berkeley and the university campus. John Galen Howard designed the central axis of the campus to align with the Golden Gate. The axis is the large open space in the middle of the campus. The axis is at an oblique angle to the surrounding streets.

The branches of Strawberry Creek join in the large forested eucalyptus grove. The curving arch of trees south of Sather Tower outlines the south branch. Trees also define the north branch, cutting across mid-campus from the north.

Aerial

In 1908 George Lawrence probably took the first aerial photograph of Berkeley using his famous Lawrence Captive Airship. He connected 17 kites with piano-wire to fly a giant 49-pound camera 1000 feet over Berkeley. He used electricity to activate a mechanism that moved the lens across the camera, exposing a very large glass plate.

George A. Pettitt's classic history *Berkeley: the Town and Gown of It* features the photograph on the inside of its cover. The photo looks east over a sparsely settled midtown toward bare hills and a cloudy sky. A dense forest fringes the university. The city is filling up, but there are still large open tracts of land. The rounded hills and the broad alluvial plain gently sloping toward the bay dominate the city.

The collision of immense tectonic plates formed the land we see from the air. Like the Ohlones, we are dancing on the edge of the world where geological titans clash. The Pacific plate strikes and slips north along the North American plate. The massive play of forces fissures and wrinkles the land. The soft, sedimentary stones of the Berkeley hills were once the bottom of a shallow sea thrust up by the collision.

A block of earth between the San Andreas and Hayward faults fell while those on either side of it rose, forming the valley that would become the bay. Throughout these dramatic events, the Sacramento River persevered, making its way through the Golden Gate and onto a low plane before emptying into the Pacific near today's Farallon Islands. At the end of the last ice age, about 11,000 years ago, the sea rose creating the bay.

The Great Central Valley was once a vast lake emptying into Monterey Bay. Tectonic forces channeled the drainage to the Carquinez Strait, releasing a flood of water and sediment into the bay, which became a shallow estuary. Later, hydraulic gold mining in the Sierras washed away mountainsides and choked the bay with sediment. Hydraulic mining was outlawed in 1883, but it took the bay more than 80 years to recover.

Protruding up from the rounded contours of the Berkeley hills are angry volcanic punctuation marks such as Indian Rock. Bay Area volcanoes arose when the Pacific plate changed from diving underneath the North American plate to slipping alongside it. Today Washington's Mount Saint Helen is testament to this powerful process.

For hundreds of generations, the Ohlones lived on the shore of the estuary. The land was covered with tall thin-bladed bunch grasses with scattered oaks along the streams. Salt- and fresh-water marshes intermingled along the ill-defined shoreline. The constant flow of fresh water into tidal surges created a great blossoming of life. A sand-spit beach backed by a marsh occupied the northern portion of the shoreline. Later, the level margin of the estuary became a perfect right-of-way for the Southern Pacific Railroad. The tracks roughly define the original shoreline.

The Spanish displaced the Ohlones and brought invasive European annual grasses that replaced the native bunch grasses. The first farmers grew great tracts of "bonanza" wheat on the rich alluvial soil until they exhausted it.

The early industrial community of Ocean View grew up around a long wharf that projected into the shallow bay. The infant college community grew independently at the base of the hills. The city developed along steam and, later, electric trolley lines radiating out from Oakland.

Above Sather Tower, better known as the Campanile, rises before an ensemble of red-roofed scientific giants. Physics is in nearby LeConte Hall and its outlying buildings. Tan Hall in the upper right is part of the Gilman Hall chemistry complex. Much of 20th-century scientific history took place in these buildings.

Mathematics' and Statistics' Evans Hall is to the left. The much-criticized "Brutalist" building fronts on the barely-visible Mining Circle. Behind Evans Hall are the graceful arches of Hearst Memorial Mining Building. The artful 1907 gem stands in strange contrast to its monumental neighbor.

Below The UC Berkeley Art Museum fan of cantilevered galleries spreads out from a central open space flooded with natural light. Visitors circle around a central ramp to the unfolding galleries. The unsupported extremities of the galleries and airiness of the construction seem to take reinforced concrete to its structural limits.

Three decades after its opening, engineers deem it beyond the limits of safety for a building a few hundred yards from the Hayward fault. It now seems probable that the museum will be relocated to the downtown Arts District.

Above A sudden gust of wind ripples the surface of Tilden Park's Lake Anza. The WPA created the lake in 1938 to irrigate the nearby golf course. They dammed Wild Cat Creek and flooded one of the highest waterfalls in the region. Amid steep hills and a verdant forest, the small lake draws crowds of bathers on warm sunny days.

Below Early land developers conceived of the Claremont Hotel as a destination for a Key Route electric trolley line. Construction began in 1906, but the ambitious project was not completed until 1915. New owners painted the building brilliant white so that it could be easily seen from the 1939 World's Fair on Treasure Island. Although widely perceived as part of Berkeley, the hotel is just over the city line in Oakland.

The Berkeley Marina and Eastshore State Park
are constructed entirely on landfill. The edge of the
park on the picture's right margin is close to the
original Berkeley beach shoreline.

The Berkeley Wharf projects far into the shallow bay. University Avenue near the Marina covers
the original wharf. Hard spots created by the old
pilings corrugate the street's eastbound lanes.

Bancroft Way is between the university campus and the Art Museum. Durant Avenue is between the museum and four high-rise dorms surrounding a central commons building near the lower left of the picture. The complex is prosaically named Unit One. It and its sister, Unit Three, three blocks down Durant, are part of the university's effort to quickly provide student housing in the decades after World War II.

The university's rapid expansion southward displaced the existing community and spawned a radical backlash. In 1969, when the program demolished an entire block of historic buildings for Unit Four, activists brought the project to a halt by commandeering the space for People's Park.

Telegraph Avenue terminates at the campus. The junction is at the crowded crosswalk on Bancroft Way about a third of the way down from the top of the picture.

Above Behind Berkeley's Beaux Arts city hall is the blocky, utilitarian police station. It was replaced by a parking lot in the summer of 2001. Hidden in the foliage to the left of city hall is a plaque commemorating the fallen soldiers of the Grand Army of the Republic — World War I soldiers.

Below Walden School on McKinley Avenue and Dwight Way is marked by colorful rectangles of yellow, red, green and blue. Further down McKinley are another private school, Berkwood-Hedge, and Washington School, which is public. Berkeley High is two blocks away. Since the founding of the university, central Berkeley has been a magnet for education.

Although the seasons are muted, every fall many trees, including the sweet gums of McKinley Avenue, put on a colorful display before dropping their leaves.

Above California Memorial Stadium (1923) is cut into Charter Hill at the head of Strawberry Canyon. It is a Roman coliseum combined with an elliptical earthen bowl. It was built over the Hayward Fault with expansion joints at the north and south ends to compensate for earth movement. The western side of the stadium is steadily creeping north at the rate of about a centimeter a year, creating prominent displacements. Massive retrofitting is needed.

The International House (1930) with its prominent nine-story dome is directly in front of the stadium at the head of Bancroft Way. The architecture is Spanish Colonial and Mission Revival. It was deeply controversial at the time of its opening. Many objected to a co-educational dormitory that included Americans, foreigners and people of color.

Below The Hearst Memorial Greek Theatre is directly north of the stadium. Residential Stern Hall is on the left and Bowles Hall is on the right. The university built the Greek Theatre in a natural amphitheater that seniors used for Class Day performances at the end of the 19th century.

The Edible Schoolyard's neat garden beds occupy an acre at the edge of Martin Luther King Jr.
Middle School's asphalt playground. Chez Panisse's
celebrated Alice Waters conceived of the idea of
growing, preparing and eating healthy food as part
of the school curriculum. Subsequently, the entire
Berkeley school district adopted the same policy.

Berkeley High School is marked by its distinctive round Community Theater building and its red track and green playing field. A new building has replaced the parking lot and low buildings along Milvia Street. The parking structure on the lower right no longer exists. The white, flat-roofed building across the street from the playing field is Washington Elementary School.

Above Glendale-La Loma Park is nestled in a residential hillside on the site of an old quarry. The intimate baseball field is a picturesque site for Little League games. In 1923 a grassfire burned through this general area and swept downhill towards Shattuck Avenue and the university. It burned much of hillside Berkeley, including a great many Maybeck houses.

Below Downhill from Glendale-La Loma is the Codornices Park baseball field. To the left of the field is the covered Berryman Reservoir (1877) built on Codornices Creek. The reservoir is located close to the Hayward fault and is at risk of catastrophic failure during an earthquake. Across Euclid Avenue from the park are the concentric tiers of the Berkeley Rose Garden and its red and green tennis courts.

Beginning at the lower left of the picture,
Ohlone Park stretches east along Hearst Avenue.
The city created the park on land cleared during the
construction of the BART tracks running below it.
Two blocks to the right of the park is heavily trav-
eled University Avenue, which terminates at the
university. Downtown and the civic center buildings are also visible.

Above Willard Park with tennis courts, baseball field and swim center is shared with Willard Middle School. A cluster of mostly flat-roofed buildings is the school. The institutions are named after the 19th-century feminist Frances Willard. During the Vietnam War, activists renamed the park Ho Chi Minh Park.

Like many Berkeley parks, an active community group supports Willard. By 1990 the park had become run-down and a magnet for illegal activity. The Friends of Willard Park reclaimed it through trash removal, landscaping and community vigilance.

Below Marin Circle is the center of the Northbrae neighborhood. In 1907 its developers promoted this area as the site for the state capital. They enthusiastically named most of the surrounding streets after California counties. The next year voters rejected the scheme, but the beautifully landscaped neighborhood remains.

Below San Pablo Park's (1914) Frances Albrier
Community Center are two sandy play areas. Nearby is one of its two baseball fields. By the 1930s the
area had become a multi-ethnic neighborhood. The
park was home field for both Oakland's and Berkeley's black baseball teams since Oakland did not allow blacks to use the city's facilities.

The photograph is of the university's historic central campus, as seen from above the hills.

At the lower left of the picture, a meandering line of trees marks the route of Strawberry Creek. The meadow surrounded by trees near the edge of the picture is the Faculty Glade. The baseball diamond is Evans Field.

The central axis of the university on the right side of the photograph is aligned with the Golden Gate. It begins at Mining Circle, which has a dark inner disk. The large open lawn on the right is Memorial Glade, named in memory of faculty, students and staff that served in World War II. Both Evans Hall below the Glade and the Moffitt Undergraduate Library above it intrude on the open axis envisioned by architect John Galen Howard.

Steps carved into the volcanic formation ease
the ascent to the top of Indian Rock. The rock is also known as Northbrae Rhyolite. A long footpath
rising from Solano Avenue leads to the park.

The stately heart of the university is framed by the Campanile and the Doe Memorial Library, both designed by John Galen Howard. Between the two is the Bancroft Library, part of a mid-century annex. The skylights in front of the library buildings are for the massive underground Gardner Stacks. The masterful Doe Library, replete with intricately spaced columns and Beaux Arts ornamentation, dominates the campus' central glade. In the university's early days, the glade was an exotic botanical garden and the school's second building, North Hall, stood in place of the Bancroft Library.

Campus

In 1856 Horace Bushnell scoured the Bay Area to find a new site for the College of California away from the rowdiness of saloon-ridden, gold-rush Oakland. Retired sea captain Orin Simmons' ranch had great appeal because of its natural beauty. It was located in the area of today's Greek Theatre and the stadium. Backed by picturesque hills and framed by the meandering branches of Strawberry Creek, the land lay directly opposite the Golden Gate. It commanded vistas of sweeping beauty: gently sloping wheat fields, scattered oaks, wandering creeks and the shimmering, island-studded bay.

At first the site was thought to be unsuitable because of the lack of water, but Simmons convinced the trustees that the creeks could be dammed and springs opened. We may think of the university campus flowing out of the bounty of Strawberry Creek, which still defines its landscape. The campus is Berkeley's loveliest park and grandest public space. Despite the urban throb of a world university, there are still graceful glades and bucolic groves.

Fortunately, the nation's most influential landscape architect, Frederick Law Olmsted, proposed the first college plan. He advocated planting trees, enhancing the creeks and orientating the campus towards the Golden Gate. Piedmont Avenue, north of campus, is the only physical vestige of the plan, but his ideas persisted. It is hard to imagine today's verdant university campus as he first saw it, an arid grassland, bereft of trees.

The university's first building, South Hall, and its sister, North Hall, were aligned with the Golden Gate. Today a line drawn through Mining Circle, Memorial Glade and the Crescent bordering Oxford Street passes through the center of the Golden Gate. Although recent development blocks much of the view, the north tower of the Golden Gate Bridge, framed by university buildings, can still be seen from the steps just west of the Campanile.

At the turn of the 20th century, Phoebe Apperson Hearst was the university's fairy godmother. She funded an international competition for a new architectural plan. Bernard Maybeck promoted the undertaking, and when the winner refused to reside in Berkeley, he recommended John Galen Howard as supervising architect.

Howard's eclectic Beaux Arts buildings define classic campus architecture. They are monumental structures characterized by granite facing, colonnades, decorative flourishes and red tile roofs with copper skylights. Other structures, such as the Greek Theatre, the Campanile and Sather Gate, testify to his versatility. In 1924, a few years after he vehemently disagreed with locating the stadium at the pristine mouth of Strawberry Canyon on an earthquake fault, Howard's contract was cancelled.

Although Howard's aesthetics continue to dominate campus, the building boom after World War II, fueled by increased enrollment and ascendancy of big science, spawned a number of reinforced concrete mid-rise monoliths. Ten-story Evans Hall and the charming Moffitt Undergraduate Library block the open space aligning with the Golden Gate. Other recent buildings, such as the Haas School of Business, are innovative and graceful. Open space has continually given way to new buildings. Nonetheless, one can still spend a pleasant hour in relative isolation on the banks of Strawberry Creek.

The campus is a crossroads of the world and the focal point of Berkeley. It is a magnet for former students. Every space has a name and a history.

45

The Class of 1910 Bridge crosses Strawberry Creek in the Goodspeed Natural Area, which is dominated by live oaks and coast redwoods. The storied Faculty Glade lies on the other side of the bridge's Beaux Arts Roman arch. Its Latin inscription commemorates the class and thanks Phoebe Apperson Hearst for her support.

Sproul Plaza is a tumult of sounds, people and political advocacy. A street musician beside Ludwig's Fountain entertains the crowd. The fountain is named after a beloved dog that frequented it in the '60s. Until mid-century, when the university acquired the land south of Strawberry Creek, Telegraph Avenue and campus-oriented businesses occupied this space.

The Hearst Gymnasium for Women is the only finished building of a large complex planned in commemoration of Phoebe Apperson Hearst, benefactress and regent of the university. It is the work of Bernard Maybeck and Julia Morgan.

Large planter boxes with Greek women bearing garlands flank the second-story outdoor pool. In the foreground are a sculpted urn and cherub.

Student dancers frequently practice in Lower Sproul Plaza directly in front of Zellerbach Hall. Piazza San Marco in Venice influenced the plaza and its placement among the surrounding student services buildings. Below the plaza is underground parking.

The campanile at Piazza San Marco similarly inspired Sather Tower, Cal's Campanile.

Beginning at Piedmont Avenue, the three wings of the Haas School of Business flow down a moderately steep slope and around an informal courtyard. The school's prominent arches, ubiquitous angles and textured surfaces, in combination with recessed and protruding bays, create a procession of fresh architectural perspectives. The informal elegance of the buildings, along with the flowing courtyard, is a late 20th-century architectural triumph.

In the foreground of the photograph is a winding handicapped ramp, at the upper end of the landscaped courtyard. It artfully represents a dry creek bed that symbolizes Strawberry Creek, which flowed through the hillside occupied by the school. The arches of the school's western gateway support a bridge that connects the classrooms of Cheit Hall on the right and the Student Services Building. The sculpture Folded Circle Trio is a compact counterpoint to the angular school.

The school is the eastern gateway to campus. It is beautifully designed to create a community of scholarship and business.

Above Rain or shine, the Circle of Concern silently protests the university's support of nuclear weapons-related research. Every Sunday for more than 20 years they have steadfastly stood at the Addison Street entrance to campus.

The university has a proud history of achievement in fundamental physics that began with E. O. Lawrence's invention of the cyclotron. However, nuclear weapons are the dark side of sub-atomic research.

Below In the last decades of the 20th century, a spontaneous gathering of community drummers occurred every Sunday in lower Sproul Plaza. Their synergistic music is a surging, pulsating rhythm.

In the new century the amorphous group migrated to the Ashby BART Flea Market, where its energetic percussion enlivens the colorful marketplace.

The monolithic Valley Life Science Building introduced Moderne and Art Deco elements to the traditional Beaux Arts style of the early campus. The north entrance, pictured above, is part of a massive renovation in the early 1990s. The building now houses elegantly designed scientific facilities that belie its Moderne exterior.

In the background are the Life Science Annex and the west campus Eucalyptus Grove. The trees were planted as a windbreak for an early oval track on the same site as the Annex.

Above South Hall is the first building started on the new University of California campus. The university's founding spirit lives in its stately elegance.

By mid-century it had fallen into disrepair and its future was in doubt. As the university's and the building's centennial approached, the administration resolved to save the structure. A series of restorations refurbished the venerable hall and installed innovative earthquake retrofitting.

Below Built in the middle of the 20th century, Sproul Hall echoes the classic Beaux Arts architecture of central campus. The building and its plaza are the birthplace of the Free Speech Movement (FSM) of the early 1960s. For reasons that seem unfathomable amidst today's unrestrained advocacy, the university attempted to restrict political speech. The students rebelled en masse and occupied the building. Speeches by student Mario Savio galvanized the demonstrators.

Today Sproul Hall's steps are named after Savio, and there are an endowed FSM Café and Archives in the library complex.

Right The belfry of the Campanile offers sweeping views of the campus, Berkeley and the extended Bay Area. It hosts 70,000 visitors a year. Each side has three high arches which are divided by ornate double columns.

Left The 61 bells of the university carillon progress from the 11,000-pound Great Bear Bell. The first 12 Sather bells were cast in England and ran the German blockade during World War I.

The Campanile, or more formally, Sather Tower, is the symbol of both the university and of Berkeley. On clear days the city's most prominent landmark can be seen from across the bay. Jane Kron Sather funded it as a memorial to herself, just as she funded Sather Gate as a memorial to her husband, Peder Sather.

The slender tower tapers inward three and a half feet from its base to its belfry. It then becomes a vertical shaft up to the pyramidal spire. A lantern tops the spire and sculpted flames terminate each of the four corners. Images invoking the "light of knowledge" are frequent motifs in early 20th-century university architecture.

The Campanile is built on the site of a revered flagpole which was the center of early campus life. The pole was situated among the first three major university buildings, South Hall, North Hall and Bacon Hall, of which only South Hall survives.

Coach "Pappy" Waldorf is the university's only statue of a person. His teams dominated post-World War II football with three appearances in the Rose Bowl and seven victories over Stanford. He was a charismatic figure who defined collegiate male virtue.

The placement of the statue became notorious when a San Francisco Chronicle article in 1998 characterized him as ogling the explicit anatomy of *The Last Dryad* across the Faculty Glade. Subsequently, the *Dryad* was subtly altered to be less controversial.

The graceful *The Last Dryad* by Alexander Sterling Calder is nestled at the edge of the Faculty Glade. The university has never been comfortable with its explicitness; for 20 years it resided in a courtyard of the Hearst Gymnasium for Women. The photograph was taken before the statue was slightly modified to blur labial definition.

On the Old Art Gallery, in a hidden corner of campus, beside Strawberry Creek, are two New Deal Works Progress Administration mosaic murals. *Music and Painting* is pictured here. *Sculpture and Dancing* is on another panel.

They adorn the exterior of one of the oldest buildings on campus. Initially, it was the Power House, supplying the rising university with electricity and steam. A few years before the murals' creation, the administration converted the building into an art gallery. After the university opened the Art Museum on Bancroft Way, the building housed minor administrative offices. Perhaps in yet another life, these patiently waiting figures will call art and music back.

Sather Gate, with its bridge over Strawberry Creek, is the traditional entrance to campus. Before the university expanded south of the creek in the middle of the 20th century, it defined the university's boundary. High on each of the four piers are white marble panels carved with nude allegorical figures. Understandably controversial, for most of the gate's first 70 years they were hidden in storage.

Strawberry Creek flows through the Grinnell Natural Area and Eucalyptus Grove at the western edge of campus. These quiet groves between the bustle of downtown Berkeley and the crowds of central campus have gladdened the hearts of pedestrians for well over a hundred years.

On the campus, the north and south branches of Strawberry Creek are mostly open and protected by natural areas and landscaping. After the branches join in the Eucalyptus Grove, the creek is culverted — with few exceptions — for the rest of its journey through Berkeley.

The towering Eucalyptus Grove was planted in 1877 as a windbreak for the historic Cinder Track just to the east.

The towering hoppers of the Berkeley Ready
Mix and Berkeley Asphalt Companies are by the
railroad tracks. Today west Berkeley is diversified,
but there are still many heavy industries.

The gammasphere is housed in one of the concrete "caves" of the 88-inch cyclotron building. It has 110 exquisitely sensitive detectors for measuring gamma rays from rare nuclear processes. Scientists use the cyclotron to create large artificial nuclei that emit gamma rays. They do this by smashing a beam of particles into a target. The new nucleus is highly unstable, but in the brief moment before it decays, the gammasphere collects data about its internal structure.

Lawrence Berkeley Lab

Since World War II, science has had an unprecedented influence on our culture. Researchers associated with the Lawrence Berkeley National Laboratory wrote much of the scientific history of the 20th century. The dome of the 184-inch cyclotron building is visible throughout Berkeley. Historically, it is one of the most important facilities of the 76-building complex. It is a monument to the lab's remarkable achievements and its current leadership in the scientific world. Originally conceived to house an immense cyclotron before World War II, it now contains the otherworldly Advanced Light Source (ALS). It produces highly engineered light one billion times brighter than the sun.

The lab's preeminence can be illustrated by elementary biology taught to every child — photosynthesis. Melvin Calvin received the Nobel Prize in 1961 for describing the role of chlorophyll in this process. He is one of nine lab scientists that have earned the Nobel. Other achievements include the discovery of 15 chemical elements. Berkelium (BK) is the only element in the periodic table named after a city. Lab scientists have discovered numerous sub-atomic particles including the antiproton and antineutron. Founder E. O. Lawrence and his brother, a physician, started nuclear medicine and first used it to treat their mother for cancer.

Lawrence founded the lab with his invention of the cyclotron in 1931. A cyclotron is a device for rapidly accelerating charged particles such as electrons through a circular vacuum chamber. The particles are energized and directed onto a circular path by powerful magnets. The cyclotron opened the door to high-energy nuclear physics. It led to "big machine science" with multidisciplinary teams of scientists and engineers. After World War II, the lab grew rapidly with federal capitalization and a succession of fundamental discoveries. Its funding for a single year can approach half a billion dollars.

This chapter includes images of the 88-inch cyclotron, a versatile third-generation machine capable of accelerating ionic beams of most elements in the periodic table. Magnets deflect beams onto different tracks — like railroad tracks — that go to research areas such as the gammasphere on the opposite page. The building is filled with gigantic interlocking concrete blocks that form experimental "caves." The beams are radioactive and require massive shielding to protect the researchers. The facility is a strange combination of foreboding medieval caves and superscience.

On pages 66 and 68 are images of the Advanced Light Source, located in the 184-inch cyclotron building. At the center of the structure is the massive magnet that once drove the 184-inch cyclotron. The magnet was too heavy to move during remodeling of the Advanced Light Source. The ALS is powered by a sophisticated cyclotron known as a synchrotron. The synchrotron accelerates a beam of electrons the width of a human hair to near the speed of light. It holds the particles for about six hours in a tubular ring approximately 200 feet in diameter. At various points, magnets agitate the beam to produce soft x-rays and ultra violet light. The light is deflected down beamlines by magnets to "endstations," where the research is done. This type of light has extremely short wavelengths. To study objects at the atomic level, scientists must use light with wavelengths the same size or smaller than the subject. Crossing the threshold of the building feels like stepping into the 22nd century.

For more information visit www.lbl.gov.

The control room of the 88-inch cyclotron has the dated ultra-high technology style of the 1960s. Before the extreme miniaturization of electronics that characterized the computer revolution of the late 20th century, instruments, processors and switches had to be housed in huge semi-permanent cabinets. The photograph shows half the control room.

The 88-inch cyclotron pipes a beam of charged particles into the Berkeley Gas-filled Separator, which sorts out various isotopes of an element. An isotope has an atomic weight different from the most stable form of an element, because it has a different number of neutrons. The silver separator sits between giant yellow magnets which deflect isotopes of different mass onto different paths.

The stainless steel tube running horizontally across the middle of this photograph is one of the 28 beamlines radiating from the synchrotron at the Advanced Light Source. It leads to an x-ray microscope used for a great variety of biological research projects. Among the many topics investigated is the structure of proteins with special properties such as making bacteria drug-resistant and regulating the growth of nerve cells.

In front of the dome of the Advanced Light Source are the original support buildings for the 184-inch cyclotron known as Old Town. The 184-inch cyclotron building was begun in October, 1940, but was not completed until after World War II. In the distance is a tower of the Golden Gate Bridge.

The stainless steel machine is a powerful vacuum chamber. It can remove virtually all the air from the high-energy conduits of the Advanced Light Source. The electrons in the synchrotron ring must travel in a sealed tube with a nearly 100% vacuum. This is also true of the intense light channeled through the beamlines.

Where once Ohlone Indians followed ancient paths to harvest grass seed, a bucolic valley of science nestles in the hills. In the foreground is a major electrical substation dedicated to the Advanced Light Source's huge demand. In the background on the left is the renowned National Center for Electron Microscopy. The microscopes can see the space between atoms.

A researcher contemplates the view from the
plaza just outside the entrance of the Advanced
Light Source. The structure behind him is the
fourth floor of Building 2, which contains material
science labs. Even the stodgiest scientific literature
refers to the Berkeley hills setting of Lawrence
Berkeley Lab as "romantic" and "beautiful." In the
background are Richmond, Brooks Island, San
Francisco Bay and Mount Tamalpais.

The Berkeley pier traces a dashed line across
the bay, separating the silhouettes of San Francisco
from bucolic César Chávez Park. Sailboats make
their way home as strollers enjoy the last of the day.

Quarterback Justin Vedder prepares to pass as aggressive Bears block the Stanford onslaught. In the background, photographers with big 400-mm. lenses line the end zone.

Cal's success in the 101st Big Game in 1998 depended on Vedder's passing. Throwing to leading Pac-10 receiver Dameane Douglas, he ranked seventh in the team's all-time passing yards. But it was not to be. Stanford's defense won the game, 10 to 3, despite 24 Vedder completions.

The Big Game

The passions of the Big Game far exceed its athletic significance. The traditions, lore and myths of Cal and Stanford are woven into its history. Both of the Bay Area's world-renowned universities regard the event with profound seriousness. Only warring siblings in a bitter moment can emulate its emotional intensity. The game is a mixture of partisan hate and regional love.

UC Berkeley sprang from Yale traditions, while Stanford has Harvard roots. Berkeley delights in its democratic inclusiveness, while Stanford takes pride in its aura of superiority. The Berkeley band and mascot pay homage to a traditional formal style, while Stanford revels in its anti-band and anti-mascot caprices. In a region with little history compared to the academic East Coast, are the raw emotions of the Big Game any wonder?

Red and white mice in Bancroft library? Cardinal red paint on the Big C above the stadium? Dire warnings from university administrators? It must be Big Game week. The meat-and-potatoes prank of the past is today's felony. Inevitably, the politicization of moral issues in the last half-century has criminalized traditional boys-will-be-boys tolerance.

However, what ambitious collegian can resist the call of immortality for a clever prank? What university administrator does not remember the deplorable violence of the past? There is a standoff between the extralegal and the once-a-year contest. But after the game, both siblings will stand together to defend the Bay Area.

The Big Game began in 1892 in a San Francisco sandlot. Berkeley says future president Herbert Hoover forgot to bring the ball, while Stanford contends both teams forgot. After a long delay and a horseback ride to a sporting goods store by its owner, the game commenced.

Seven years later, Stanford cheerleaders brought a lumbering axe to a baseball game in hopes of spicing up a traditional collegiate chant about axing the opponent's neck. It proved so effective that after Stanford won, a mob of Berkeley students stole it. A legendary chase through the streets of San Francisco ensued. As police searched for the thief at the ferry to Oakland, a wily student cut off the handle and smuggled the axe aboard in his clothing.

Berkeley retained possession of the axe for decades until 21 enterprising Stanford students using strong-arm tactics melodramatically raided an armored car. Another wild chase followed. Both schools celebrate these felonious assaults. The axe changed hands illicitly many times. Eventually, officials tried to end the illegality by making it the Big Game trophy.

The photographs are from the 101st Big Game of 1998. Berkeley was in the middle of a seven-game losing streak. Cal's last moment of legendary glory was its incredible upset victory of 1982. That year, in the last seconds of the game, "The Play" made its twisted way into collegiate history. The Stanford band ran onto the field for a victory celebration as the Bears took a kickoff and made a series of five laterals while weaving through the band for the winning touchdown.

In 1998 Berkeley students stole the Stanford tree and held it hostage until administrators went ballistic and the tree was meekly returned.

See http://ucrc.berkeley.edu and http://www.stanford.edu/group/axecomm.

Cal cheerleaders delight; Cal mascot Oski surveys the game benignly; and the leader of the band looks on with deep concern. The traditions are all here — heart-stopping glamour, storied equanimity and collegiate intensity.

Cheering Cal students passionately thrust their pom-poms into the air. They are participating in a hundred-year-old tradition. One of the non-traditional T-shirts in this photo is digitally altered to extend hair over the letter k.

The blue and gold California banner first appeared in 1895 when California's conquering track team toured the East Coast. One side of the banner pictured a golden bear. The banner and a song celebrating it created the golden bear as the university's guardian.

The university honors seniors with a bouquet of blue irises and golden roses. Left guard Kevin Swillis' solemnity and humility reflect hallowed traditions. On page 72 he can be seen blocking for quarterback Vedder.

The Big Game draws a huge multi-generation crowd to California Memorial Stadium. Behind the Cal players is their gold-dusted rooting section. The standing Cal and Stanford players anxiously follow every play from the 50-yard line.

Charter Hill rises behind the five-story stadium. It is colloquially known as "tightwad hill" for the fans that want to watch the game but would rather not buy a ticket. Charter Hill is also the site of the Big C and the California Victory Cannon. Almost 70,000 paying spectators attended the 101st Big Game.

The Tree dances with a cheerleader. Stanford's guerilla-chic cheerleading style, featuring grenade belt and red beret, is the antithesis of Cal's short skirts, open midriff and pom-poms. Stanford does not have a mascot, despite appearances. The Tree is a band member who only looks and acts like a mascot. Stanford's symbols mock tradition.

Amid swirling cheerleaders' skirts, Oski greets his enthusiastic fans. Oski never speaks, never reveals the identity of the person inside the suit. Only Oski is real. He embodies the spirit of generations of Cal students.

Originally the spirit of Oski dwelt in live bears brought to early athletic contests. In 1941 he was reincarnated in his present form. The name derives from a turn-of-the-century yell: "Oski wow wow! Whiskey wee wee!"

The clash and flash of cymbals by the identically-uniformed Cal marching band shows off the pride and spirit of its traditional formalism. The picture was taken at the 1997 game against Oregon.

The Stanford band does not march in formation. Nothing is too flamboyant or outrageous for this highly entertaining group. It breaks every rule of formal expectation. Like the Tree, an anti-mascot, it is an anti-band, mocking convention and originating new styles.

Both bands contradict the popular impression of their universities. The formal style of Cal's band opposes the perception of the university as diverse, egalitarian and liberal. Stanford's band belies the school's traditional homogeneous, elitist and conservative image.

Above After losing the game, Cal students charge toward the Stanford bleachers. Seniors would never have a Big Game victory. Emotions run high, and a faux mini-riot is traditional. Security staff form and hold the line, but cannot prevent the clods of dirt from arcing toward the celebrating, taunting Stanford students.

Below Stanford men also know how to take off their shirts and paint themselves. They throw their emotions into every second of every play.

At dusk the Cal Band marches out of the coliseum to minister to the raw emotions of the Cal partisans. They lend a sense of majesty to Piedmont Avenue and the residential streets north of campus. The band holds its head high and plays school songs with the solemnity of a hundred-year-old tradition. Go Bears! Next year Oski will axe the Tree. In 2002 Cal finally won.

Berkeley police gather at dusk in front of the new Public Safety building. They are preparing to escort the Critical Mass demonstration — a parade of bicycle riders that would soon invade the streets. The first police chief, August Vollmer, initiated bicycle patrols.

Telegraph Avenue ends at Sproul Plaza, where traffic flows onto Bancroft Way, the southern border of UC campus. Most of the buildings visible were built before World War II. The original campus business community began here in the 1870s at the corner of Choate (Telegraph) and Bancroft with a hotel, rooming house, restaurant and grocery store.

Telegraph and its thriving community of small businesses originally extended to Sather Gate until the businesses on the east side of the street were replaced by Sproul Hall in 1941. Twenty years later the businesses on the west side and the street itself were replaced by the California Student Center and Sproul Plaza.

Before and after the Free Speech Movement, the area was frequently the site of protests and demonstrations. Precariously perched on a board resting on a five-gallon bucket atop a camp-stool, a lone protester rails against the loss of UC Berkeley Chancellor Chang-Lin Tien.

Tien was a popular leader from 1990 to 1997. He was admired for countering the loss of state support through successful fundraising and for vigorously opposing the Regents' dismantling of affirmative action. The protester's sign begins, "God doesn't like—Chancellor Tien getting the sack."

Telegraph

The first telegraph to reach the West Coast threaded through the hills and canyons along today's Claremont Avenue and on into Oakland. The Pony Express followed the same route but became obsolete with the completion of the telegraph in 1861. The road alongside the wires was named Telegraph. Later the route that connected the boarding houses in Oakland to the new University of California inherited the name.

The Berkeley campus was to be a pastoral gem financed by the sale of lots south of Strawberry Creek. The street leading to today's Sather Gate was named Choate after a noted physician. When instruction began in 1873, a horse-drawn trolley brought students to the rural campus.

Telegraph Avenue and its side streets thrived. Early in the 20th century, large four- and five-story brick buildings were built with small shops at street level and housing above. For more than a hundred years, students created an insatiable demand for housing, meals, books, entertainment, art, fashion and sundries. A procession of small businesses rose and fell, keeping the Avenue fresh and exciting. By the 1930s it had developed a bohemian and intellectual image.

The cultural climate inspired by the university's academic and social openness has given Berkeley a long history of passionate social activism. When the children of the mass middle class that emerged after World War II revolted against cultural hypocrisy, Berkeley became a focal point of the youth revolution. The Free Speech Movement (FSM) flamed to life in 1964 when the university attempted to limit free speech. Student Mario Savio proclaimed that the university was part of a machine that had become so odious that "…you've got to put your bodies upon the gears…you've got to make it stop…un-less you're free, the machine will be prevented from working at all." Over the next decade, racism, Vietnam, imperialism and gender and sexual liberation kept Telegraph Avenue burning.

Throughout the 20th century the university expanded south of Strawberry Creek. After World War II, it began acquiring large parcels of land south of Bancroft Way for student housing. Community resentment grew as entire blocks were demolished and replaced by high-rises. Activists brought land acquisition to a halt in 1969, when they proclaimed that a demolished block of housing east of Telegraph Avenue was People's Park. When the university fenced in the property, thousands of people marched on the park and confronted the police. For two weeks the neighborhood was a battleground. The governor declared martial law. One person was killed and hundreds were injured or arrested. Three years later, the fence was torn down and the park restored, but the issue has never been fully resolved.

Telegraph became a counterculture cauldron. For a few years after the FSM, social activists, flower children and hippies mingled. Amid the ferment of ideas the Avenue was friendly and exciting. But by 1968 it changed with the introduction of methamphetamines and other hard drugs. Since that time, the neighborhood has been troubled by drug dealers, the homeless and disaffected youth.

Telegraph is the great attractor of intellectuals, students and tourists. Its business community is in perennial conflict with the untidy aspects of street life. Periodically the city attempts to regulate the mercurial conflict with new laws. Police presence has increased and become more sophisticated and community-oriented.

The sculpted steel and glass of Bear Basics reflects Telegraph's busy street life and invites it in. Its modern openness and glass exterior are in stark contrast to the fortress mentality adopted by businesses during the riot years of the 1960s and '70s.

The street's vitality springs from its social and architectural diversity. Bear Basics and other contemporary structures share the street with nearly 100-year-old large brick residential buildings with small shops at street level.

The bricked-in windows of Bank of America are a legacy of revolutionary Berkeley. The colorful T-shirts with fractal images of the '60s and '70s offset the bank's formal stamp-like logo.

Telegraph street vendors cater to the incessant crowds of tourists with artifacts of the counterculture. Occasionally street commerce is so intense that the Avenue is closed to motorized traffic to accommodate holiday crowds.

Hippie Hairwraps
① CAN be removed without cutting hair.

The artist Twig weaves colorful, intricately textured creations such as necklaces and belts. His hairwrap is based on bracelets that are woven around strands of thread instead of hair. Unexpectedly they became symbolic of the Avenue's innovative artisans. Personable Twig enjoys the interaction with customers and their appreciation of his art.

The pictured Hippy Hairwrap is the first in a series of models that are periodically retired due to weathering.

Telegraph is a venue for many unique artists. The incredible intricate wire weavings of A. W. Michael Thomas have supported his family for 20 years. The powerful woven-wire head sells for four figures. Lesser creations are inexpensive.

Students and intellectuals from throughout the world gather at Caffè Strada for espresso drinks and pastries. Soft classical music drifts through the murmur of languages as students study and argue and laugh. Most of the seating is outdoors beneath flowering pear trees in fenced alcoves lined by benches.

Strada is between International House and the University Art Museum. It is two blocks from Telegraph on Bancroft across from the Anthropology Museum. The atmosphere is cultured and sophisticated.

In 1958 the espresso revolution in Berkeley began in Caffè Mediterraneum. For decades the Med was packed with artists, intellectuals and political activists. The partisans who created People's Park mingled with poets and writers. It was a busy countercultural crossroads where an eclectic mixture of people had lively discussions. People hung out for hours.

In recent years the Med has become more sedate. Its patrons have aged and many have moved on. But it is still a pleasant place to drink espresso and watch the passing parade.

Above On weekends vendors line the street with tables. The sidewalks fill as crowds of tourists seek easy entertainment. Inexpensive jewelry and hanging baubles are very popular.

Telegraph has an irresistible attraction to Berkeley kids when they reach their early teens and start to go about town on their own. It offers great people-watching, dozens of fascinating stores, affordable trinkets and an abundance of cheap eats. After a while it loses its luster, but all of Berkeley occasionally visits the area's extraordinary book, music and specialty stores.

Below Crowds of students and tourists swirl among islands of camped-out street people. There are always knots of people sitting on the sidewalk engaged in various activities from panhandling to chess.

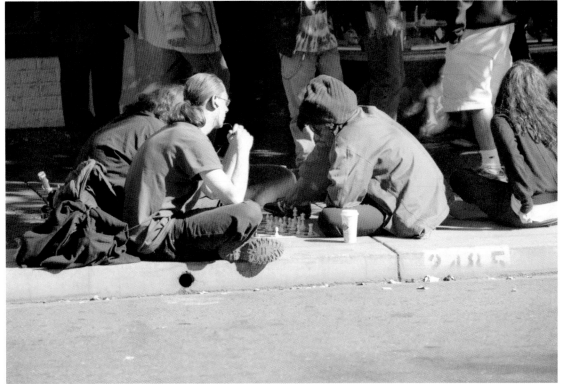

Early in the morning as the city wakes up, street vendors begin setting up their tables on the Avenue. Each vendor is assigned a space along the four blocks that comprised old Choate Street.

The rich cultural atmosphere of Telegraph extends into its cross streets. For instance, a Durant courtyard is filled with tiny Asian restaurants representing half a dozen countries.

Telegraph is abuzz with activity. People and bicycles weave through traffic. An unconventional youth and a bearded old-timer chat beneath the street sign.

For well over a hundred years, a great university has electrified the street. A major thoroughfare alive with action abruptly ends at its historic destination.

The natural beauty of People's Park belies its
reputation. Early in the morning many of the
habitués gather at its eastern end along Bowditch
Street to catch the first warmth of the sun.

In Berkeley a Victorian couple would plant two palm trees in front of their cottage. Today magnificent trees stand before aged houses. Janet Berrien captures them by painting a wooden panel passionate red. Then she layers on and scrapes back intense acrylics to achieve her design. The process cracks the surface, suggesting private stories hidden behind the image.

Artists

On a fine April day in 1860, the trustees of the College of California gathered to dedicate a new site at a rocky outcrop near the banks of Strawberry Creek. Eight years later the College would become the University of California. They looked over a gracefully sloping plain filled with wheat and dotted with majestic oaks. The mighty Pacific Ocean lay beyond San Francisco Bay and the Golden Gate. Standing on the rock, trustee Frederick Billings was moved to recite from the poetry of Bishop Berkeley, "Westward the course of empire takes its way…" Six years later, at Billings' suggestion, the trustees named a proposed community adjacent to the college "Berkeley."

Since its inception in poetry, fine artists and craftspeople have thrived in Berkeley. The city is a magnet to artists for many of the same reasons that attracted the trustees — delightful climate, natural beauty, nearby urbanity and easy transportation. Its culture is rooted in learning and art.

Barely visible in 1860 along the Bay shore was the commercial and industrial settlement of Ocean View. Its robust development throughout the city's history created a fruitful tension with the visionary university community. Today many nationally prominent artists have studios in West Berkeley. Some occupy former industrial buildings while others have live/work spaces. Aside from the beauty of its location, Berkeley attracts artists because of its artistic vibrancy, intellectual intensity and political engagement. The city is culturally diverse but has a cooperative tradition.

The renowned California College of Arts and Crafts began in 1907 near the western edge of the university campus. Twenty-three years later it moved to better facilities in nearby Oakland, but it still maintains strong ties to Berkeley.

The arts are a thriving industry in Berkeley. For a city with just over 100,000 people, the statistics on artistic and cultural activity are staggering. The city estimates art annually generates a quarter billion dollars in economic activity and reaches an audience of 1.8 million people. There are 16 museums, at least 23 festivals, a major recording studio, a film industry, a rich literary tradition and hundreds of fine artists and craftspeople.

The city government is aggressively promoting the downtown Addison Street Arts District. Embedded in the sidewalk just below Shattuck Avenue are ten full-size art panels, 120 plaques of Berkeley poetry and a meandering ribbon of red concrete. Major museums and cultural institutions such as the University Art Museum, the Pacific Film Archive and the Lowie Museum of Anthropology may migrate into the district.

Ceramicist Nancy Selvin, one of the seven artists featured in this chapter, comments on Berkeley's artistic ferment: "I identify with this community. I think it's more of a psychological identity than is actually represented in the work, because being here, you just sense a tremendous freedom. You can make anything you want, do anything you want. There aren't certain boundaries on what can be made in clay, and that concept grew out of this area, Southern California and out of the Bay Area. I think you really sense that, and when you go into your studio, you feel that sense of freedom to just work on anything you want, go in any direction you want… You have to create your own identity and that's wonderful… In that sense there's that regional sort of love of being here as opposed to places that I think are more conservative about what should or should not be done, what is art and what isn't."

Nancy Selvin is a nationally recognized ceramicist whose work is in the Smithsonian Institution as well as numerous other museums and private collections. She has been recognized with national awards and presents workshops both here and abroad. She is involved with community service projects that span the country from the Bay Area to Maine.

Above The first step in creating the notebook series is to pour a clay slurry into a negative mold of a book held in a styrofoam base. Here Nancy lifts the clay book from the mold.

Below The clay book is painted with a broad brush. Nancy's distinctive brushwork and layered composition are signatures of her work.

One of the layers in Nancy's ceramic books is silk-screened fragments of text or drawings. They are hints of ideas about making art. She takes them from a journal-like collection of ideas maintained since her student days. The compositions are a public version of her private book.

Her art is domestic. It is an intensely personal and universal discourse on the history of domestic places and life.

Berkeley is rich in accomplished ceramicists. Down the block from Kevin Nierman's live/work studio is Robert Brady's TRAX Gallery. A few blocks north is Nancy Selvin's studio. Many artists locate between the freeway and San Pablo Avenue from Harrison Street into Emeryville. This stretch of land is Berkeley's Ocean View industrial area. When industry declined, artists moved in.

Although nationally respected for his work, Kevin is best known in the Berkeley community for his teaching studio, Kids 'N' Clay, where 200 kids a week freely express their creativity in a nurturing atmosphere. A book of the same name has brought his ideas to an international audience.

Kevin is standing by three of the four panels of his massive *Shard Wall*. This is the second version of the wall, the first being too massive to move from the studio. He is best known for the cracked pot series. It features expertly thrown pots that are broken and given individual Raku firings and then reassembled. They symbolize each individual's life being broken and reformed into a new creative whole. The *Shard Wall* series is an evocative embodiment of the same idea.

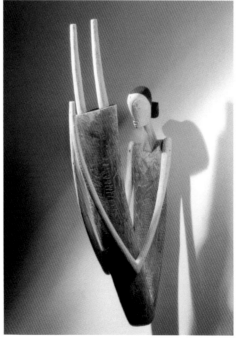

Eclectic sculptor Robert Brady exhibits and lectures throughout the country. His work is in prestigious museums and has won national awards. More significantly, he is an important influence on a generation of ceramists. For over 15 years he has carved wood, such as the startling life-size figures pictured here. He and his functional potter wife, Sandra Simon, opened the TRAX gallery beside the Southern Pacific Railroad tracks near Gilman Street almost a decade ago. Recently they built a live/work space for the gallery near the trendy retail shops on 4th Street.

Robert's austere wooden carvings occupy a space between the human form and an intense spiritual vision. He does not consider them "angels," but it is a word that readily comes to the mind of many viewers. He plays with the proportions of the human figure, using sparse dramatic forms. The sculptures' emotional power is created by the tension between the metamorphosed human elements.

Jody Fine's glass art is widely collected. He takes great joy in his technical mastery of ancient Venetian glassblowing techniques. Much of his art, such as the *Face Cups* being crafted here, has a functional basis. Other works are whimsical recreations of real objects such as a cherry pie or a prickly pear cactus. His stunning marbles are world famous. He believes glass reflects the artist's personality. The swirling, exuberant colors of his pieces mirror a playful delight.

Above Jody attaches the nose to a *Face Cup*.

Below He heats the finished cup before very slowly cooling it in a kiln.

Opposite Jody blows air into molten glass through a hollow tube — a punty — to begin the cup. He then twirls the punty like a baton to elongate the glass. Red-hot furnaces glow in the background. They are used initially to melt the glass and then periodically to reheat the pieces during the creation process.

102

Glass artist Mary White and her craftsman partner, Jerry Sears, live in a West Berkeley 1882 landmark house remodeled into a live/work residence.

White is pictured with a reverse painting, *Wisdom Wall*. Ginkgo leaves are sandblasted onto the back of the panel. Then they are filled with oil paints, gold leaf and other foils. The back of the panel is painted blue, making the front radiant with reflected light. The Italian-German technique dates back to the Middle Ages. Ginkgos are ancient trees whose leaves are thought to increase mental ability. Mary believes our culture must seek wisdom. The painting is meditative, meant to calm the mind with the interplay of leaves, color and light.

She works only with recycled materials. A passionate environmentalist, she believes that artists don't necessarily need to use new materials. She restores used glass and scrap steel to a new beauty. The glass house on the opposite page is made from used plate glass that has been cut into bricks, smoothed in a rock tumbler and glued together. Other houses are made by firing recycled glass or melting it in a kiln.

Mary is best known for her glass house series, "The Wanderers and Seekers." She began the project when she acquired and restored her Berkeley home. She had moved frequently and wanted to explore our need for a place, for a special context. She exhibits the houses in groups to create a sense of community. All are illuminated from within. She believes with the Quakers that every being has an inner light, every house a spirit. In addition to her environmental concerns, Mary is an organizer within the arts community.

Jerry Sears turns "pieces of ideas" into "pieces of furniture." He is a master California artisan who starts with a concept and realizes it in textured wood. He is also a fine artist. In the background of the previous page is the stick figure sculpture, *Evilution, a Nuclear Family with Family Values*. In 1958, while in the Navy, Jerry witnessed 22 nuclear tests on the Pacific island of Eniwetok. *Evilution* has odd parts, appendages and cooling tower heads, his vision of our nuclear future.

He is in front of the cabinet *Back East*, which is inspired by this fourth-generation Californian's first visit to the East Coast. The quilted maple and tiger maple reds at the top represent the pervasive heat. The orange of the spalted maple drawers stands for the smell of rust and decay. The dot-lined strip of gold at the bottom expresses constant cell phone connectedness. Jerry points to a bear he bought in Sabeao, Japan, in 1958, after the nuclear tests.

Behind him is the *Little Head* cabinet made of wood from The Heritage, President Andrew Jackson's Tennessee estate. The wood is spalted hackberry that blew down in Hurricane Hugo in 1989. The spalting occurred over many years, as the decaying tree absorbed minerals while still standing. "Little head" is construction slang for $20 bills. "Big head" is for $100 bills. One is Jackson, the other Franklin.

The beauty of a sunset over the San Francisco
Bay and the natural landscape dwarf man-made
structures. The vast expanse of the estuary provides
respite from the cities crowding its shores.

The "Joe Camel Anti-tobacco" mural appeared from about 1999 to 2003 directly opposite the doors of the Berkeley High School gymnasium. The student group ART — Artists Resisting Tobacco — painted it with the assistance of muralist Corinne Cuiney. The artists' names appear beneath the list of carcinogenic chemicals.

The mural's arresting style and vibrancy are reminiscent of the motifs of underground comics. The striking central image and surrounding vignettes infuse it with emotional power. Tragically, it was destroyed to make way for new construction.

Murals

The Mexican muralist Diego Rivera was fascinated by the card stunts at a 1930s Berkeley football game. He thought they were living murals. Over 40 years later, he and other Mexican muralists of the period would inspire an explosion of outdoor murals in Berkeley. Rivera did not paint a mural in Berkeley, but he did use the city's internationally acclaimed tennis champion Helen Wills Moody as the model for his *Allegory of California* in San Francisco. The countercultural murals, beginning with *A People's History of Telegraph Avenue* (1976), are deeply indebted to his allegorical style and political consciouness.

The Mexican muralists led the way for the Works Progress Administration (WPA) artists who painted graphic stories in thousands of public buildings during the New Deal. There is a small example on the west wall of the main Berkeley Post Office. Unfortunately, McCarthyism caused many WPA works to be painted over, and public murals went into a hiatus.

The blossoming of protest movements in the late 1960s reinvigorated the art by using outdoor walls as political bulletin boards. Activists spontaneously began painting political slogans and cartoons on an inviting wall just west of People's Park known as the *People's Wall* (c. 1969). The bicentennial celebration in 1976 inspired Osha Neumann and others to transform this space into *A People's History of Telegraph Avenue*. The loose group of artists brought together by this project created the dominant Berkeley style with a series of major murals executed over the next five years. *Telegraph Avenue* is a Berkeley historical landmark, but most of their other murals have been painted over or destroyed. Their style is characterized by strident countercultural values and widespread community involvement in the creation of the art.

During this same period, whimsical murals with no overt political content began to appear. They were usually by single commissioned artists. An early example is Anodea Judith's *California Poppy House* (1975), which can be seen on Parker Street (page 146). Huge orange flowers resembling poppies grow from a drainpipe stem, and a sculptural butterfly perches on the roof. Stefan Adams' surrealistic *Dutch Boy* (1974) on University Avenue was less fortunate. It was painted over when the building changed hands. It featured an image of the Dutch Boy logo painting a view of San Francisco Bay from a high ladder. Fortunately, the era's most accomplished whimsical mural, John Wehrle's *ancisco* (1978) still exists at Santa Fe and Gilman Streets. It blends panels of the San Fr"ancisco" Bay mudflats with realistic features of its host building, the Toot Sweets Bakery. The mural was repainted with major modifications in 1995 by Wehrle and remains vibrant.

In recent years, murals celebrating the Berkeley community's history, life styles and values have joined the two earlier traditions. New outdoor murals frequently blossom with fresh energy, youthful vitality and color. Over time, they become part of our daily lives, reflecting our culture and brightening our journey. But time and weather are not kind. Colors fade, content becomes blurred, accidents occur, graffiti obscures and our old friends slowly diminish. Often murals are thoughtlessly destroyed when buildings are repainted or demolished. Fortunately, some classic murals have been restored. And art is breaking out everywhere at the dawn of the new century. We are enjoying a renaissance. Architecture, sculpture, sidewalk poetry, fine arts and performing arts have joined the movement spearheaded by the muralists.

Before Europeans arrived, well before the inception of European culture, the peaceful Ohlone people lived in Berkeley. Jean LaMarr's *Coyote Creation Story* (1995) poetically expresses the unity of the people and the land's natural abundance. The mural is one of four depicting Ohlone history on a large BART ventilation building in Ohlone Park.

Gracing La Peña Cultural Center, *the Song of Unity* (1978) celebrates the cultural richness of the Americas. Depicted in high relief are the face, arm and severed hands of singer Víctor Jara. He bled to death leading a stadium of junta detainees in song during the 1973 Chilean coup d'état.

The mural's three-dimensionality is created by papier-mâché, ceramic elements and a slight outward curving at the ends. Created by Ray Patlan, Brian Theile, Osha Neumann and Anna de Leon, it is part of the same tradition as *Telegraph Avenue*.

John Wehrle's 1978 rendition of *ancisco* covered the entire wall of the bakery building with a surrealistic panorama of mudflats and bay. The 1995 mural recreated the scene but as a reflection in the bakery's windows. All the brick and tile work is painted to match the front of the building. Depicted in the three major panels are *Mudflat Reflections, Time and Tide* and *Wooden Dreams.*

Larry Todd's delightful *Rat and Dinosaurs Play-ing Cards* (1998 to 2002?) is an evolutionary caution tale. The crafty rat wins everything, but the di-nosaurs keep playing until they are driven to ex-tinction. Todd is also known as underground car-toonist Dr. Atomic. The mural was located at Gilman and 10th Streets until the building was de-molished.

Simeon Pelenc created the library's treasured
sgraffito panels in 1931 by the ancient art of layer-
ing different-colored plaster and incising the top
layer to reveal the underlying colors. In the 1950s
they were painted over and forgotten, victims of the
same aesthetic that destroyed WPA murals.

The panels were accidentally rediscovered and
restored in 1973. In 1997 they regained their full
glory when the library was repainted its original
deep green. Today they are considered Egyptian,
but in 1931 they were thought to be Mayan.

Artist JoeSam is renowned for his celebration of African-American culture. His sculptures have a joyful exuberance of color and action. These sculptural murals are on satellite buildings at the Berkeley Alternative High School.

He was born in Harlem and earned a doctorate in education. For the last 20 years he has devoted himself completely to art. His sculptures enliven public spaces throughout the Bay Area.

Based on a design by Osha Neumann, *A People's History of Telegraph Avenue* (1976) was created by Janet Kranzberg, Brian Thiele and Daniel Galvez, along with hundreds of others. It was financed by funds collected on site in a can. Painted by a variety of political and community activists, it is the quintessential "community mural."

Above left The Free Speech Movement's Mario Savio speaks in front of Sproul Hall.

Opposite page Disintegrating columns spew bombs and dollars into a montage of political figures and protesting activists. UC President Kerr, caught between cultures, clings to a column.

Above left Unplugged TV culture melts into colorful Telegraph Avenue street life. The Bubble Lady is next to a man unraveling on LSD.

Above right Rebels create People's Park on UC land in celebration of life and hope.

Left On May 15, 1969, the university fences in People's Park and mass protest erupts. A police helmet and barricades face the protesters. The helmet is attached to actual electrical lines symbolizing UC and corporate control.

Right The mural is painted on what was then the Forum building at Telegraph and Haste. Protesters open a fire hydrant and fling back tear gas. A Viet Cong flag was painted on the street earlier.

Left James Rector is murdered by Alameda County sheriffs. The stark photo-realism, like many mural details, is based on documentary photographs. The sheriffs stand on a smoking, demolished helmet severed from its controlling wires to symbolize defeat of the system.

Right Out of the flames of the old system the people joyously dance into the future. Beside a homeless woman a tree erupts through concrete.

119

Children garden and play in an idyllic school-yard in front of a hillside full of flowers. The scene occupies a few feet of a 72-foot-long mural painted by about 100 children. The *Berkeley is …* mural (1999 to 2000) existed briefly at the construction site of the police and fire departments' Public Safety Building. A number of schools and youth programs painted their vision of community life under the co-ordination of the Kala Art Institute. The mural is painted on a plywood construction fence.

The city's mobile *Bicycle Mural* (1998) by Berkeley artist Tricia Tripp is painted on four movable panels. It can be transported from place to place to hide construction projects or to enliven public spaces. It was commissioned to celebrate cycling as an alternate form of transportation. In the photograph the bicyclist and pedestrian seem to have emerged from the mural.

In April 1997 neighbors were shocked that the city had painted pink one of Berkeley's classic murals. Located on the Telegraph Avenue side of Willard School's gymnasium, *Intersections* (1980) was the largest mural in Berkeley. It is the work of the same loose group of artists that formed around *Telegraph Avenue* — Osha Neumann, Daniel Galvez and Brian Thiel. Numerous Willard students and members of the larger community contributed to the mural. The project was supported by a grant from the California Arts Council. It was meant to show the vastness of knowledge and experience as it intersected with student life.

Fortunately, the city was able to partially restore the mural. To warn future generations, it now has a great sheet of pink paint peeling back to reveal a complex natural and symbolic montage.

Protesters establish a homeless camp at old City
Hall. The demonstration here and across the street
in Martin Luther King Jr. Park generated lots of
press but few solutions.

Berkeley High School's class of 1999 throws their caps into the air. The colorful graduation ceremony is sometimes solemn but more often exuberant. Beach balls suddenly appear overhead or a cloud of soap bubbles streams upward.

The Greek Theater is filled to its capacity of 10,000. As the seniors receive their diplomas, family and friends erupt into applause and yells. Many seniors demonstrate quirky performance skills as they approach the podium. At the end the audience streams into the inner circle. Everyone is hugging and taking pictures.

Events

For its relatively small population of just over 100,000 and modest size of 18 square miles, Berkeley cooks. Events surface like bubbles in a boiling pot. Art and politics thrive. There are major museums, live theaters, nightclubs and bookstore readings. Sports are huge. Chapter 5 focuses on the Big Game, the region's oldest mass event. Chapter 11 portrays the city's most exuberant and colorful new event, the How Berkeley Can You Be? parade. This chapter is about Berkeley's hometown events.

Events in socially stratified 19th-century Berkeley were divided between the bustling industrial hub of Ocean View and the emerging university traditions. Aside from politics and religion, Ocean View social life centered about restrictive clubs. The university was an exclusive enclave, but its students participated in the city's first large-scale social events.

In Ocean View informal social gatherings emerged in 1854 with the opening of Bowen's Inn and with the saloons that arose alongside factories and docks. Social clubs such as the West Berkeley Clam Club, which sponsored grand balls, formed in the 1870s. A lively succession of fraternal orders started with the Ancient Order of United Workingmen. These lodges were ceremonial secret societies. The spirit of social exclusivity extended to the invitation-only volunteer fire companies.

At the university, Senior Pilgrimage, a last tour of campus, started in 1874. It was a solemn ceremonial occasion. Every four years on February 29th, turn-of-the-century students labored with pick and shovel to improve the campus. The first Labor Day was held as a demonstration of the school's lack of funding. The era reveled in sentimentality coupled with physical exertion. However the Class Rush showed another face — the raw West's violent rough and tumble.

Following widespread academic tradition, the new university adopted the Rush. At UC the freshman class proved itself by imprinting its class numbers on a hill overlooking the next day's Charter ceremonies. The hill is above today's Memorial Stadium and Greek Theater. Sophomore honor depended on throwing freshmen off Charter Hill before they could desecrate it. There were many injuries and serious accidents. Sophomores began tying up freshmen and hiding them under bridges or behind walls. In 1905, after an accidental maiming, the university stopped the Rush and symbolically buried it under Charter Hill's newly constructed Big C. Students soon resurrected the rivalry on the playing fields with grand tugs-of-war and huge pushball contests.

Berkeley loves a party. The city's first mass venue was the Hearst Greek Theater (1903). Sarah Bernhardt hosted a benefit there for victims of the 1906 San Francisco earthquake and fire. Presidents Theodore Roosevelt and William Howard Taft spoke there. It was supplemented in the 1960s, when Zellerbach Hall became the university's premier venue.

Mass events became common in the latter part of the 20th century. In the 1960s political protests converted the streets and parks into venues. The city's diverse ethnic population and multitude of local cultures sponsored numerous festivals. Today, we have the Himalayan Fair, Indigenous Peoples Day and the Berkeley Arts Festival. In the 1970s BART made Berkeley easily accessible to neighboring cities. Visitors from throughout the region also arrive by train, bus, car, boat and bike.

Above Margaret Sullivan, flanked by Misha Stapleton and Jonathan Taylor, expresses the spirit of a Berkeley High graduation.

Below Berkeley (in white jerseys) prepares to pass. Women's Field Hockey is one of 27 varsity sports. Berkeley High may have the highest number of sports teams in the nation. One third of the approximately 3,000 students participate. In this immense school with its diverse cultures, athletics give students a social home based on discipline and camaraderie.

Point Guard Danesha Wright takes the ball for Berkeley as the opposition anxiously defends the basket. Berkeley High's women's basketball team is nationally ranked and frequently doubles the score of their opponents. The Yellow Jackets play here in Donahue Gym.

Above Both soccer teams are in the air, as Berkeley, in red-and-blue jerseys, attempts to take control of the ball. The game is at the high school athletic field.

Below The Berkeley High player in the white cap tries to score despite a clinging defensive player. The water polo match is at the Willard Pool.

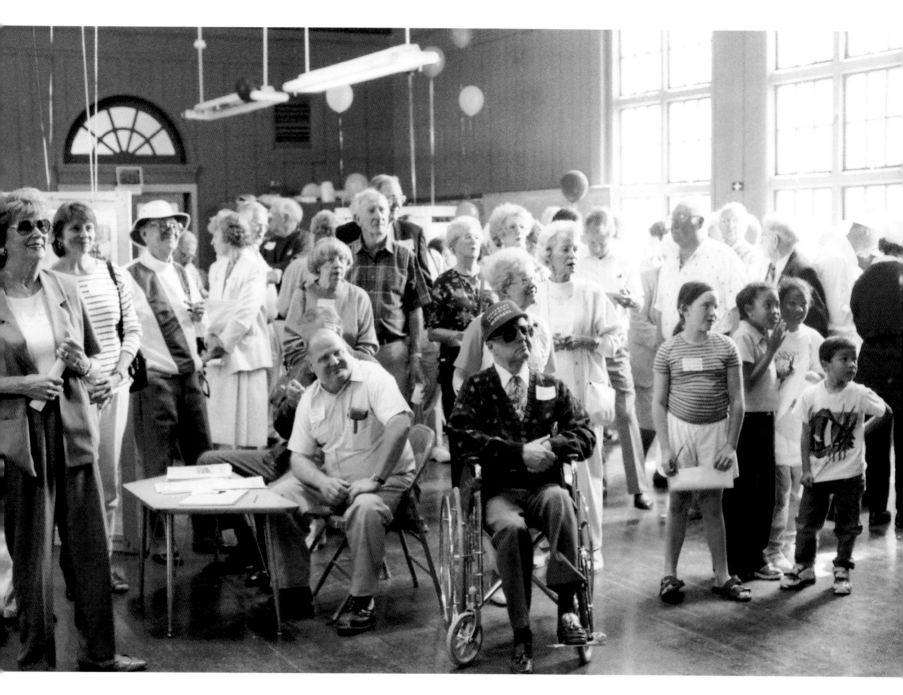

Generations of Jefferson School students gathered for its 90th anniversary. The rural elementary school was founded in 1907 under the able leadership of principal Mary O'Bannon.

Former students from throughout California attended, representing every decade of the school's existence. It was a touching tribute that enjoyed great community support.

Above The 18th century mixes amicably with the Bay to Barkers festival in César Chávez Park. This is the grand promenade of dogs and owners around the park's 1.3-mile perimeter.

Opposite About 150,000 people attend the Solano Stroll. It is Berkeley's and neighboring Albany's annual reunion where friends and classmates catch up. The stroll is by far Berkeley's largest mass gathering. The street is alive with local merchants, vendors, performance artists and community organizations.

The annual Berkeley Kite Festival fills the sky above César Chávez Park with all manner of traditional and fanciful kites. A giant scuba diver kite and an octopus kite swim through an ocean of air. Colorful wind socks, bigger than semitrucks, rotate slowly above the ground, tethered by a heavy chain.

The festival is combined with the West Coast Kite Championships. There are precision flying teams, beautifully choreographed kite dances, traditional Japanese kite fighting and a great variety of individual and team competitions.

The park is one of the world's best urban kite-flying venues. The festival began in 1958 and attracts as many as 25,000 people from around the world.

Although the Kite Festival has its serious competitive side, it is also a kid's paradise. There are free kite-making workshops and free flying lessons. There is a popular candy drop. The festival offers exotic food and artisan kite booths.

But best of all, you can stand on a hill and fly your kite in a blue sky filled with hundreds of marvelous creations.

Counter-culture icon Wavy Gravy enjoys his 65th birthday celebration held at the Berkeley Community Theater on May 15, 2001.

Wavy Gravy is a revered Berkeley character. Locally he is known for the circus and performing-arts institution Camp Winnarainbow. Nationally he is known for constant fundraising for Seva Foundation, an international health foundation dedicated to ending preventable blindness and other projects. He is always fun, always a clown, always using laughter to inspire social activism.

His Hog Farm collective is alive and well in North Berkeley. It first came to national attention as security, "the Please Force," at the original Woodstock festival. Since that time Wavy has been an active cultural ("under-the-counter culture") force. To honor his "ascension into geezerhood," the city declared May 15th Wavy Gravy Day.

Wavy Gravy may have achieved geezerhood, but Jeremy Shafer has a long way to go. Shafer has been a circus arts instructor at Gravy's Camp Winnarainbow since 1988. Here he delights a Solano Stroll audience, as he has done every year since 1987, his freshman year at Berkeley High.

Shafer is a one-man circus skilled at such prodigious feats as juggling five fireballs while riding a unicycle. Sometimes he rides a flaming unicycle. He is also an internationally recognized author and origami artist. He has made numerous television appearances in the U.S. and elsewhere.

The graveyard is in front of a magnificent Spanish Revival house on Russell Street that fell into disrepair in the 1960s. It scared neighborhood children who thought it was haunted. New owners renovated the property and began decorating for Halloween. Neighbor Pat Jackson passed out flyers in 1980 inviting neighbors to compete for the spookiest house and they enthusiastically responded.

Thousands of children are drawn every October 31st to the scariest street in the Bay Area. Every year homeowners along a two-block stretch of Russell Street west of Claremont Boulevard create ever more spectacular displays. Halloween crowds grew so big in 1993 that police closed off the street. Strolling musicians join the crowds of costumed children. The spirit of the haunted house takes over the entire street.

Opposite The Flad Family graveyard features a real skeleton glowing from within, witches and elaborate witty displays. Down the street a huge red monster reaches out for innocent little children. Sometimes flying saucers land or a giant spider preys on a child. Through word of mouth, a little neighborhood celebration became a spontaneous community event.

The Berkeley Flea Market is a cacophony of goods and music. It is an international bazaar, a grand garage sale, a gallery of African art, a food emporium and a New Age supply depot. It is a vibrant eclectic community gathering. In the shade of the Ashby BART station, 20 or more drummers weave their rhythms together in a pulsating beat that washes over the teeming parking lot.

The Flea Market is a community project that began in 1976. The organization's proceeds are donated to local groups such as the Berkeley Free Clinic and the Tenant Action Project.

The Downtown Berkeley Association's Front Row Festival blues concert fills Center Street with a casual audience. People and dogs wander about. Delighted couples dance in front of the stage. Commercial booths line the east end of the street.

Central Berkeley, with its Addison Arts District, is a fascinating, lively city center, but this was not always so. In 1990, to reverse the decline of downtown the state of California selected Berkeley as an Urban Main Street Pilot Program. The project's remarkable success can be attributed to the vitality, creativity and energy of the city.

Above Berkeley author Theodore Roszak's *The Making of the Counter Culture* (1969) announced the youth revolution. Here he is presenting a new work on the aging of the baby boomers, *America the Wise* (1998), at Black Oak Books.

Opposite Citizens gather in 2003 for a group photograph to celebrate Berkeley's 125th anniversary. Behind Mayor Tom Bates (at right in blue shirt and dark sports jacket), a figure in wig, robe and clerical collar portrays Bishop Berkeley, for whom the city was named.

CELEBRATE
Berkeley's 125th Anniversary
1878 – 2003

Thousands filled Kittredge Street to await the Grand Opening of a redesigned and expanded Central Berkeley Public Library on April 6, 2002. Thousands more toured the new facility that afternoon. Delighted patrons were eager to see how the sumptuous new building blended together with the historic 1931 Beaux Arts structure.

Keynote speaker, author Alice Walker, was adulated by an overflow crowd. Deep didjeridu tones resonated through the building. Live music filled the airy rooms. Asian lion dancers and senior tap dancers performed.

Berkeley loves a library. It has the highest per-capita usage of any California city. Residents have consistently supported the library by voting special taxes and bond measures. There are 100 Internet workstations, a new Berkeley History Room with ornately carved doors and a sunny Art and Music Room that occupies the entire fifth floor.

Prenatal Water Exercise for pregnant women is
one of many special-interest classes at the Downtown Berkeley YMCA. The family-oriented "Y" is
one of the city's most popular institutions.

Living and Growing

In 1891 naturalist and poet Charles Keeler was drawn to a man of unusual appearance on the evening ferry from San Francisco. His strange ideas challenged and provoked Keeler. For a year or more these chance meetings educated Keeler in Bernard Maybeck's unique perspective on the arts. Keeler thought he had met a young Socrates.

A few years later Maybeck designed a home to fit Keeler's personality on a hillside lot near the university. The process gave Keeler a liberal education in architecture and Maybeck a publicist. The home was the first Maybeck designed for another person. It featured redwood shingles over massive one-by-eight-foot planks mounted on giant four-by-four-foot posts. Maybeck left all the interior timbering, including the planks, exposed. He designed the house to blend with the hillside as it weathered. In a single stroke Maybeck brought the Bay Area Arts and Crafts Movement to maturity.

When Keeler worried houses built by others would destroy the effect, Maybeck told him to see that it did not happen. Charismatic Keeler recruited neighbors to build Maybeck-designed homes. The Hillside Club later grew out of this advocacy.

Keeler's *The Simple Home* is the club's statement of principles. The garden secludes the home from the street. It cloaks the house in plants and becomes another room. The storied Temple of Wings is an extreme expression of this view. Thirty-four Corinthian columns support two elliptical roofs — the wings. In place of walls, sailcloth was deployed during inclement weather. Today the verdant surrounding gardens make the exterior of Maybeck houses difficult to photograph.

Originally Berkeley's vast grassland was broken only by streaks of trees and brush along its many creeks. The city is washed by marine winds and fog that moderate its Mediterranean climate. Given water and conditioned soil, almost all of the planet's vegetation will thrive except plants of polar and desert extremes.

In 1865 college trustee Reverend Samuel Hopkins Wiley built a house south of campus. For a number of years, it was the sole dwelling on the lots set aside to finance the construction of the College of California. Wiley diligently planted trees along the streets and on campus. Over the next two decades, residents of the growing settlement planted more than 50,000 trees. By 1873 hundreds of exotic trees and shrubs grew on campus. Blue gum eucalyptus, Monterey cypress and redwoods were planted with enthusiasm. As the university community grew, a strikingly diverse urban forest emerged.

In part, the university was founded as an agricultural college. There has always been a concerted effort to bring exotic plants to Berkeley. From the 1890s, the university Botanical Gardens systematically searched the world for specimens. There were expeditions to the American west coast, China, the Andes, South American deserts and southern Africa. Individuals took up the Eden call and nurtured a bewildering array of plants. One of Berkeley's greatest pleasures is to walk the streets and enjoy its amazing and mysterious gardens.

As gardeners reveled in diversity, so did builders. The Hillside Club rebelled against the Victorian artifice that we prize today. We applaud Queen Anne and Italianate painted ladies that appalled them. Strange and unique combinations of materials and motifs continue to appear. Berkeley horticulture and architecture grew together in symbiotic and unpredictable ways.

Left A number of Berkeley houses have whimsical decorations. Artist Anodea Judith fancifully decorated a Parker Street residence with three large flowers growing on vines and a large butterfly sculpture. It is known as the California poppy house because of the shape and color of the flowers.

Right A central Berkeley house is ornamented with wisteria vines and a multifaceted roof. The driveway gate contains a subtle optical illusion.

The ARTech Building (2002) in Berkeley's Arts District helps define the area with its use of sculptural and mosaic art. Climbing the building's tower wall is Ken Kalman's copper salamander. Dimitry Grutsky's animal-form mosaic benches are strategically placed along the perimeter. The garage door is Amy Blackstone's picture in black iron, *Steel Egret Gate*. On either side of it are Fran Fegal's handsome mosaic murals, *Watershed 1: Mountain Lion* and *Watershed 2: Great Egret*.

Julia Morgan, an early protegée of Bernard Maybeck, is part of the Bay Area Arts and Crafts movement. She designed a number of Berkeley homes including the Olney House (1914) above. The earth-tone redwood shingles, exposed timbering, leaded windows and side entrance are characteristic of Morgan houses. Her nearby St. John's Presbyterian Church is now the Julia Morgan Center for the Arts. Morgan also designed the UC Greek Theater, Hearst Castle at San Simeon and the Berkeley City Club.

The bountifully paned Italianate Victorian
(1889) in central Berkeley is essentially unaltered. It
is one of the city's few remaining farmhouses, bereft
of its barn and servants' quarters. The building is
adorned with golden scrollwork beneath the eaves,
small golden protections or dentils beneath the
overhangs, ball-and-spool porch trim, finely turned
columns and windows with stained-glass panels.

Above Fan palms and birds-of-paradise frame
the stairs of a California bungalow in central Berkeley. The architectural style was popular between
1910 and 1925.

Opposite The lush growth of a fruiting banana
plant growing next to a residential street graphical-
ly illustrates the microclimate between Martin
Luther King Jr. Way and Sacramento Street.

At UC Botanical Gardens is one of the most valuable collections in the United States. There are over 12,000 species from throughout the world.

Visitors are often surprised by beauty, such as a fallen philodendron leaf lying on a bed of wild strawberries.

There is such a great variety of trees growing in Berkeley it is often difficult to identify a particular specimen. There are a few common trees but a great many more exotics. Several Chinese pistache trees are on Gilman Street near Hopkins. They are pleasant, unpresuming trees most of the year but are among the few trees that have a brilliant fall display.

Edward Niehaus' Stick-Eastlake Victorian home
(1889) and its gardens originally occupied the entire
block. The house is a showplace for intricate ornamental scrollwork produced in Niehaus' West
Berkeley planing mill. Niehaus probably designed
the house, which he built in sight of his mill.

Architect Eugene Tsui built the Ojo del Sol House (1995) for his parents based on a microorganism, the tardigrade, noted for its structural strength. The house is exceptionally strong with reinforced concrete shaped into parabolic curves. The interior is defined by rounded surfaces. A curving ramp provides access to the second floor. Ridges along the roof act as air conduits for passive heating and cooling.

Scattered through Berkeley are a number of small- to medium-sized affordable housing developments. At Ocean View Garden Apartments (1982), 62 units border the upscale 4th Street shopping district. The development is inviting with its clean utilitarian lines, setbacks and functional landscaping.

The city sponsors a large array of services to its less affluent citizens, including medical outreach to newborns and seniors, clinics, senior community centers and homeless services.

Left In 1923 Berkeley's great fire destroyed many of Bernard Maybeck's hillside homes. Afterward he began using fire-resistant material such as the stucco and red tile here. The Nixon-Kennedy House (1923) has two separate structures connected by a bridge above Maybeck's finely crafted gate.

Right Further up the hill is a recent building in the Arts and Crafts tradition built on a very steep slope.

A lone South African calla lilly rises through ferns on 5th Street.

Walking through Berkeley, one is frequently surprised by beauty — the play of light on textured surfaces, the juxtaposition of flower and leaves, the flare and filtering of sunlight through a garden, a fleeting glimpse of a rare blossom or the melding of structural detail and botanical grace.

The *Echinopsis terscheckii* cactus from Argentina dwarfs strollers in the UC Botanical Garden's New World desert region. The Mexican fan palm (*Washingtonia rubus*) trunk and lower leaves are in the middle ground. Blue-green *Paya venusia* from Chile are in the foreground.

The gracious garden is Berkeley at its loveliest. It is unmatched in its verdant riparian setting, burgeoning biological diversity and breathtaking beauty. The Golden Gate Bridge is visible through resplendent foliage. The Rhododendron dell in bloom is unforgettable. The Japanese Pool astride Strawberry Creek is furnished with artifacts from the 1939 San Francisco World Fair. The Tropical House, Fern and Carnivorous Plant House and the Arid House nurture plants not suited to Berkeley's climate.

The Botanical Garden is an apt symbol of the city's biological, architectural, cultural and social diversity.

The Schultz House (1892) is a beautifully maintained example of Queen Anne Victorian style, which features lavish ornamentation covering the exterior.

Bernard Maybeck rebelled against the exquisite detailing and architectural flourishes exemplified by the Schultz and Niehaus houses. Today both styles are admired.

In a tableau of Berkeley, the First Congregational Church's steeple rises between the towers of the Unit 3 student housing complex. Commercial buildings dominate the foreground.

The electric couch, chair and end table come from the protean imagination of electrical engineer Greg Solberg and designer Lisa Pongrace. They are seated on the left side of the couch. In subsequent parades Greg and Lisa drove giant pink bunny slippers and motorized cupcakes.

At Burning Man in 1995 they saw people sitting on plywood being towed by a truck. Solberg and his friends devised the electric living room as a more stylish mode of desert transportation. Their extreme art cars are built on frames powered by golf cart motors with furniture set on top.

How Berkeley Can You Be?

The parade's name, How Berkeley Can You Be?, is a challenge. Berkeley becomes a state of mind. The parade displays the city's uniqueness. The land directly across from the Golden Gate is blessed with an independent spirit and a caressing Mediterranean climate. The bucolic setting nurtures pervasive intellectualism, artistic license and inventive commercialism. The city has a ferment of people and ideas. The standard "The People's Republic of Berkeley" and "Berzerkeley" draw attention to the city's singularity, but How Berkeley Can You Be? lets all the chickens loose.

People from throughout the Bay Area join the parade and participate in the anarchistic art of being "Berkeley." The parade draws many of the same groups as the Burning Man Festival, Art Car West Fest, Gay Pride Parade and Carnival San Francisco. The enigmatic Extra Action Marching Band and the Caribbean dance group All Ah We are from Oakland. The idiosyncratic Cacophony Society and acrobatic Cheers are from San Francisco. Inventively sculpted, painted and decorated art cars come from throughout the region.

The parade's "no is yes" and "yes is no" ethos can be disturbing. When People Eating Them Animals (PETA) offers spectators delicious grilled dog, fistfight violence stalks the float. When the naked Explicit Players share the street with serious Brazilian dancers, hostility rages. When Young Republicans for Heterosexuality march, confusion reigns. Are they real or a spoof ? Billionaires for Bush is classic. But Vulva University is hypersexual, too funny, damn clever or way too over-the-top. If you have a category, forget it; everything is its own creation. The parade is an offensive, hilarious, heartwarming and visually stunning mix.

There is also hometown Berkeley. The public library marches with the Over 60 Health Clinic and the Berkeley High Jazz Band. More staid members of the community also join the parade: the mayor, city councilpersons and the United States Representative. Local celebrities such as Wavy Gravy, Jeremy Shafer, the Pink Man, Joseph Charles and Country Joe McDonald are crowd favorites.

The parade began in 1996 when merchant John Soloman of Caffe Venezia sought a way to boost the image of University Avenue. Today the street's commercial district is an active part of the general rebuilding of downtown, but at the time it had become somewhat seedy. Soloman thought a parade would draw people to University Avenue and promote its reawakening. It could celebrate the city — its cultural richness, diversity and vitality.

Soloman's inspiration was Pasadena's Doo Dah Parade that revels in irreverence and the weird. Doo Dah is a reaction to the formalism of the Rose Parade and is advertised as being unstructured. But no city can shed structure like Berkeley. Doo Dah does not allow motorized vehicles or nudity, strictures that don't apply to the How Berkeley Can You Be? challenge. Nudity plays a very small role, but motorized vehicles — fantastic creations of all kinds — are about half the parade.

Each year the parade draws more photographers. It is a living kaleidoscope of color, action and eccentricity. Some groups are especially photogenic. The fantastic carnival costumes of All Ah We are featured in four photographs. Creative Rene Soloman, son of John, appears in two photographs, the Grass Suit and Young Republicans for Heterosexuality.

Cheers San Francisco is an eclectic acrobatic group with strong ties to the gay and lesbian community. At each major performance they pass spirit buckets for donations to aid people with life-threatening conditions. Their extreme athleticism is fearless. Here they are doing flying stunts directly above the asphalt of University Avenue. They perform at an impressive variety of venues.

The Extra Action Marching Band has none of the disciplined wholesomeness of Cheers. A thunderous drum section and a boisterous horn group are set off by the explicitly sexual, gender-bending antics of the flag team and pep squad. They are outrageously attired in raunchy costumes. The band often gives impromptu performances and aggressively engages audience members. Their chaotic spontaneity inspires a strange, lurid fascination.

The amorphous 40-plus group is based in two Oakland live/work warehouses. In part it began as an offshoot of San Diego's performance art group Crash Worship. But it also grew out of the same artistic and anarchic sensibility that inspires the San Francisco-born Burning Man Festival. Performances are blatantly over-the-top. The only things treated seriously are music and ideas.

Left For 40 years the San Francisco Mime Troupe has performed in basements, parks and premier venues. They use mime in its root sense of mimicking with satire. The activist performance group has toured Europe and America and won many prestigious awards.

Right Gloria Baker 1921-2004. The Gray Panthers are persistent social activists. Baker sashayed her skirt throughout the strenuous parade route.

Left If you want to be a parade standout, wear red or perhaps pink. Unknown violinist.

Right Nothing is pinker than Pink Man. He is an emotional guy with acrobatic control of his unicycle. He darts through crowds with swallow-like dexterity. There are moments of high showmanship. Pink is an intense state of mind.

Michael Max tried out a pink dance costume on the University of Oregon campus. People called out, "Pink Man!" and a star was born.

Left The Cacophony Society float of the dead reclaiming their property from affluent yuppies. The enigmatic image is both disturbing and compelling. The society promotes a zone of perception defined by incongruity and surprise. Sometimes posted on a Berkeley telephone pole is one of their prank posters advertising a book burning or psychic car repair. The front of the float appears on page 176.

Right Unknown violinist. The striking understated elegance of the silver-faced violinist graced the parade for a number of years.

Left Ivy Okasako of the Caribbean dance group
All Ah We. The dance and drum ensemble began in
Berkeley and has since moved to Oakland. The
name is a West Indian term meaning "all of us" and
reflects the group's cultural inclusiveness. The pulsating music and stunning costumes derive from
the exuberant Caribbean carnival which began with
the injection of African ritual and dance into European carnival traditions.

Right Nancy Melville of the Brazilian carnival
dance group, Mara Reggae.

Every year the City of Berkeley funds the participation of the refuse collectors. They march in the parade and clean up the park after the parade and festival are over. They are pictured bedecked with balloons waiting for the start of the 1997 parade.

The Potala Palace, the traditional residence of the Dalai Lama, is Tibet's largest monument and most sacred site. Berkeley's Tibetan Association of Northern California constructed this replica.

There is a strong Tibetan presence in Berkeley with the Himalayan Fair in Live Oak Park and five commercial businesses. The association works to free Tibet from the Chinese occupation.

Middle school girls wielding lawn mowers chase a living grass suit down University Avenue. Rene Walker Soloman made the piece by spraying a suit with adhesive and coating it with grass seed. Nature and art worked their magic to create this tour de force.

Soloman based the hilarious stunt on a similar performance in 1981 by artist Gene Pool. Pool went on to cover cars and a bus with grass. Even though Soloman's art is derivative, it shows stunning creativity in a high school student.

Caffe Venezia manager Carol Agrimson helps recover a huge plate of spaghetti after a direct hit by a giant meatball hurled by a catapult. The young volunteer may be rethinking his decision. Caffe Venezia is noted for its creative decorations and enthusiastic participation in the parade. Owner John Soloman is father of Rene and the parade.

Left Glen Thum of All Ah We. The Caribbean Carnival tradition is famous for huge elaborate costumes constructed with gossamer material floating on loops of durable wire.

Right Kelly Anderson of the Brazilian dance and music company Ginga Brasil. They specialize in traditional and contemporary Brazilian dances. The Berkeley-based group has performed in Asia, Brazil, Europe, the United States and the Solano Stroll. Talented Conceicão Damasceno is its founder and artistic director.

Left Where are the Fashion Police when you need them? Mark MacDonald gives you his head on a plate.

Right Ruby Abrams of the Fashion Police is presumably writing a ticket for wearing too much beige. The five other officers who patrol the parade also give tickets for reckless coordinating, loitering with clothes on, sandal permit not prominently displayed, bad hair day, reckless accessorizing and dressing to incite parental distress. Headless MacDonald is perfectly within his rights.

Left Limmie Sims of the Caribbean dance group All Ah We. Giant masks are part of the African tradition of Caribbean carnival.

Right The front of the Cacophony Society float of the dead rising up to reclaim their property from the living. The back of the float is on page 168.

These vaguely disturbing bizarre figures are the signature of a society that specializes in disharmonic gestures and events. It delights in cultural dissonance.

Above The irrepressible Garry Golightly, otherwise known as Bubbleman, dips eight badminton rackets into a five-gallon bucket of solution and spins around to send clouds and clouds of bubbles into the air. Kids are in awe.

He keeps up a constant chatter from his DOTCALM van. After a while he says, "I'm going to do it again. I'm going to do it again." He jumps out and soon the air is filled with bubbles and kids are scrambling in the street.

Golightly lives in Seattle because its moist air is ideal for making bubbles the size of a small elephant. He is a fixture at Seattle children's parties, where he preaches the virtues of really cheap toys.

Below The Wave costume, a Peter Minshall "dancing mobile" worn by the executive director of All Ah We, Suzanne Ludlum. Minshall is an award-winning costume designer from Trinidad. The All Ah We Caribbean carnival dancers are among the most photogenic groups in the parade.

Left In the mid-1990s downtown Berkeley looked much as it had in the 1940s but had deteriorated. Moderate Shirley Dean, mayor of Berkeley from 1994 to 2002, greatly advanced the area's rehabilitation. Today's thriving Arts District and new mixed-use mid-rises have their origins in her administration.

Right City Councilmember Dona Spring promotes rehabilitation of the city's warm pool used by elderly and recovering citizens. She is a strong advocate for progressive social causes.

Left Creative Rene Walker Soloman stymies parade-goers with "Young Republicans for Heterosexuality." Well-dressed Berkeley High School friends hand out little pills.

Right Barbara Lee cast the sole congressional vote against military action in Iraq. In 2002, as her car rolled along the parade route, it was accompanied by a wave of hearty and continuous applause. Many local celebrities are warmly greeted, but there has never been an affirmation like the crowd's emotional response to Lee.

In 1976 Ron Dolce covered a girlfriend's car with brushed-on white paint. A few years later he began an eighteen-year project by outlining the car with marbles. The car's surface is flawlessly covered with stained glass. Dolce is a trained artist with a notable sense of design, color and craftsmanship. The Glass Quilt Car is the art car genre's premier example.

In the 1970s and 1980s a number of isolated individuals began creating art cars. The city's earliest example was a dirt-filled pickup in North Berkeley that grew vegetables and flowers. The Cloud Car is another early example that can still be seen on the street. Ron Dolce remembers seeing a VW bug with a key protruding from the rear.

About the same time Dolce began his journey, Harrod Blank started metamorphosing a VW bug into what eventually became an encrusted collage of symbolic memorabilia, the Oh My God! Car. Blank's obsession with art cars led him to produce two stunning photography books and two videos. He is an acknowledged leader of the art car movement, if such a populist art can be said to have a leader.

The Camera Van is Blank's greatest work. He is standing on the van, camera in hand, next to Coleena Hake, creator of the Doll Car. It began when Blank tried unsuccessfully to capture viewers' initial reactions to his first art car. He had a dream about a car covered with cameras that would provoke and record viewers' reactions. It took two years and some advice from Ron Dolce to turn the dream into the triumph of the Camera Van. The vehicle is amazing to see on the street, and it just might be recording your reaction.

Above Anti-war and veterans activist Country Joe McDonald has been a Berkeley resident since the 1960s. He has always been musically and politically active. He performed his famous "I-Feel-Like-I'm-Fixin'-to-Die Rag" at Woodstock. The chorus still resonates:

> And it's one, two, three,
> What are we fighting for?
> Don't ask me, I don't give a damn,
> Next stop is Vietnam

Below A temporary and clever art car, Y2K Bug makes fun in 1999 of the media hysteria about the effect of the year 2000 on computer programs. White-uniformed people attempt to exterminate the bug by spraying the crowd with water. The car and the giant parking meter are creations of local Berkeley artist and man-about-town Jim Rosenel. Parking meters are a sore point in Berkeley. People hate them and during this period vandals had decapitated almost every meter in the city.

A procession of art cars brings up the rear of the parade. As using cars to express dreams and fantasies became more prevalent, the movement extended to motorcycles, bicycles and other self-propelled vehicles. A giant guitar motorcycle, a banana-shaped bicycle and a self-propelled Red Radio Flyer wagon have been part of the parade. One of the most creative examples is the self-propelled baby bassinette. Perhaps it is a statement by an unknown wheelchair artist.

In 1949 pacifist Lewis Hill founded Berkeley's
KPFA as the nation's first listener-supported station,
with a strong bias toward participatory democracy.
Fifty years later the national Pacifica Foundation
fired KPFA's general manager, imposed an on-air
gag order and locked out the staff.

A shantytown of protesters occupied the street
in front of the station. Ten thousand people
marched through Berkeley in the largest demonstration since the Vietnam War. Part of the 1999 parade was a small but emotional echo of the march
held two months earlier.

For decades a modest garage on Roosevelt Avenue has proclaimed a simple patriotic message: "God Bless America." Later, the dates 1776 and 1976 were written vertically on either side of the doors.

A toppled Monterey Cypress planted by the WPA frames two strollers along the bay's original shoreline. Aquatic Park contains freshwater wetlands, salt marshes and tidal mudflats. Thirty-two species of marine birds visit, including California brown pelicans, Canada geese, cormorants, egrets, grebes and herons.

In recent years thousands of volunteers helped create a children's castle-like fantasy playground and climbing structure. The city recently completed a gracefully curving pedestrian and bike bridge across I-80 to connect the park with the Marina.

Parks

Until the early 1900s, Berkeley abounded in open farmland and undeveloped hillsides. In 1903 the Key Line network of electric trains and ferries opened the city's neighborhoods to San Francisco commuters and ignited a building boom. During this period there was a nationwide pattern of real estate interests extending interurban trains to their undeveloped suburban holdings. The boom intensified when 10,000 to 20,000 people took refuge in Berkeley after the 1906 San Francisco earthquake and fire. Many stayed and a great number of businesses relocated here.

Concerned with the rapid loss of open space, Berkeley dedicated its first public park in 1914. San Pablo Park is to this day immensely popular. Since the Hillside Club leased water company land and created Codornices Park in 1915, citizen advocates have financially supported parks and volunteered their labor. Over the next few years the city and its residents created nine other parks, but the total area was only 45 acres.

Despite this meager beginning and lack of urban planning, Berkeley now has a rich variety of parks. Accidents of history and a fortuitous geography intervened to mitigate the lack of city planning and the commercial lust of the 1900s.

Until 1929, when water from the Mokelumne River in the Sierra foothills was brought to Berkeley, the city was starved for water. Private water companies bought and protected the East Bay hills watershed very early. The state later converted these assets into the East Bay Regional Park District. Wildcat Canyon, adjacent to Berkeley, became its first park. Tilden Park is a marvel with its Environmental Education Center, Little Farm, merry-go-round, Lake Anza, golf course, pony rides, miniature trains, botanical garden, picnic areas and hiking trails.

Counterbalancing the regional parks on its eastern border is the Berkeley Marina, which projects into San Francisco Bay. Although a treasured part of Berkeley, it resulted from negligence and environmental desecration. In 1924, despite the objections of conservationists, the city disposed of solid waste by dumping it into the bay.

New Deal programs greatly benefited Berkeley's parks. In Tilden Park the Civilian Conservation Corps built the golf course, the Lake Anza dam, hiking trails and picnic grounds. The Works Progress Administration (WPA) built the Brazilian Room, the Yacht Harbor and the Rose Garden (1937). They also constructed the Bayshore Highway (now the Eastshore Freeway) on bay fill. Besides destroying the original shoreline, the highway created a muddy lake south of University Avenue. The WPA created Aquatic Park (1937) in this area by installing tide gates to provide circulation while keeping the water level constant. The original shoreline runs along the eastern edge of the lake.

A few more parks were built in mid-century, but the city did not embrace urban open space until voters passed a bond measure in 1974 to acquire and construct parks. The reawakened environmentalism took advantage of an historic opportunity. Activists refused to allow BART to run on elevated tracks within the city. Houses were cleared from a strip of land along Hearst Avenue so that the tracks could run underground. The open land was converted into Ohlone Park (1979). The city now has 52 city parks occupying about 3% of its land.

Above The lagoon at Shorebird Park provides Berkeley's only beach access to the bay suitable for water play. The park features an attractive nature center built of rice straw bales. Nearby Cal Adventures offers public sailing and windsurfing classes.

Below Across a narrow neck of land from the lagoon, a forest of masts rises above the Berkeley hills. The yacht harbor has berths for nearly 1,000 boats and full facilities for servicing them and their owners. The state flower, the California poppy, blooms in the foreground.

Bureaucrats were not amused when Fred Fierstein plopped his Guardian sculpture in front of the Berkeley pier in 1985 to defend the waterfront from greedy developers. It is modeled on a Malaysian temple piece of the protective Chinese god See Jin Kooi. The god proved efficacious and Fierstein did not receive a threatened littering ticket.

The Marina's Adventure Playground is a magnet for kids. They can build with hammers and saws or climb rope nets and suspended tires. They can even cling to a pulley and zip down a suspended cable. The concept originated in the rubble of postwar Europe. Designers discovered that children preferred manipulating found materials in the dirt to using traditional asphalt playgrounds.

People in César Chávez Park see the setting sun highlight the Richmond-San Rafael Bridge for a fleeting moment. They are on a paved trail that continues around the perimeter of the park. Baby strollers, wheelchairs, bikes and dogs are common.

From 1960 to 1981 the park served as the last of the Marina's landfill sites. Today it is the city's second-largest park with hiking trails, a wildlife sanctuary and sweeping views of the bay. A prevailing wind from the south makes the park a kite flier's paradise.

A tired bicyclist relaxes at Tilden Park's Inspiration Point on the ridgeline of the Berkeley hills. It looks eastward towards the San Pablo Reservoir and land preserved for its watershed.

Charles Lee Tilden was a prominent Bay Area businessman and regional park activist. During the depression he loaned the park district the funds for its initial acquisition of land.

On many weekends Tilden's popular Lake Anza fills to capacity. Originally built by the WPA to water the park's nearby golf course, it is now Berkeley's only sandy bathing beach.

But this was not always true. Early Berkeley had an extensive sandy beach stretching from today's University Avenue to just east of Golden Gate Fields. Between the beach and the Southern Pacific tracks were extensive marshes fed by Codornices and Schoolhouse Creeks.

Berkeley's shoreline remained more or less intact until the WPA used the last of the sand to build the Bayshore Highway, which is I-80 today.

Generations of children have participated in the life cycle of cows, sheep, pigs, goats, rabbits, turkeys, ducks and chickens at Tilden's Little Farm. It has many of the same problems as commercial small farms, including rustling and lack of pasture, but has the luxury of supporting heritage breeds.

In 1955 the Kiwanis Club and Berkeley High School students built the farm to 5/8 scale.

The Brazilian Room's sun-dappled lawn is one of many idyllic picnicking areas in Tilden Park. It forms a backdrop to the popular building's many weddings and receptions.

The Brazilian government donated the room's rich interior at the close of the 1939 World's Fair on Treasure Island. The WPA built the exterior from local stone and timber.

Pheena, a life-size fin whale on the plaza of
UC's Lawrence Hall of Science, is irresistible to children. The university's many public spaces and at-
tractions complement Berkeley's city and regional
parks. Fin whales have asymmetrically pigmented
lips, half white, half black.

Modern rock climbing began at Indian Rock Park and other nearby jutting outcrops of volcanic rock in the Berkeley hills. When Mason-McDuffie developed the area north and east of Marin Circle in 1917, they donated three small parks to the city: Indian Rock, Mortar Rock and Grotto Rock. For his day, Duncan McDuffie was a committed conservationist.

In 1932 Dick Leonard, the father of technical rock climbing, formed the Cragmont Climbing Club, which was soon absorbed into the Sierra Club. Another Berkeley resident, noted environmentalist David Brower, climbed with Leonard. Techniques learned at Indian Rock were soon used in Yosemite Valley and the Sierra Mountains to achieve climbs once thought impossible.

During World War II the army called on Leonard and Brower to use their mountaineering expertise in Italy. After the war, the "Sierra Club technology," born in Berkeley and honed by wartime necessity, began spreading. Berkeley became the national center for outdoor equipment and a new local industry flourished.

Opposite Tiers of roses progressing from white to deep red rise up through Codornices Creek Canyon in Berkeley's beloved Rose Garden. Architect Bernard Maybeck suggested its design.

Above A delicate big leaf maple frames a sturdy palm in Ohlone Park.

Above After the university fenced People's Park, activists created People's Park Annex on raw land above the BART tracks parallel to Hearst Avenue. Today's Ohlone Park children's climbing structure is the last remnant of this ad hoc effort. Its freeform design is an expression of turbulent revolutionary Berkeley.

Below On weekends San Pablo Park is crowded with activity. There is organized baseball and soccer as well as neighborhood pickup football and basketball. The park has a well-utilized picnic area and an enclosed tot lot. Strollers abound.

San Pablo Park began with realtor Mason-Mc-Duffie's donation of land. During the 1930s it became a gathering place for the surrounding black community. In the 1930s and 1960s organized community pressure defeated attempts to build de facto segregated schools on park land. Its popular baseball diamonds have graduated a number of players to the major and minor leagues.

Cooling marine fog is one of the pleasures of Berkeley summers. Here it lingers in an eastern valley of Tilden Park just below Nimitz Way.

Nimitz Way is north of Inspiration Point. It is part of the 31-mile East Bay Skyline National Recreation Trail that follows the crest of the hills. The 3.5-mile paved portion of the trail is popular with hikers and bikers. Bay Area landmarks are visible in every direction. The Army originally constructed the narrow paved road for access to three Nike missile pads and a small base.

Selected Bibliography

Aronovici, John (Ed.). *Quick Index to the Origin of Berkeley's Names*. Berkeley. Berkeley Historical Society, 2004.

Barish, Mildred S. *Tamalpais Tales: A Berkeley Neighborhood Remembers*. Berkeley. Buckeye Books, 2004.

Barnett, Allan W. *Community Murals: The People's Art*. New York. Cornwall Books, 1984.

Berkeley! A Literary Tribute. Edited by Danielle LaFrance. Berkeley. Heyday Books, 1997.

Berkeley History Book Committee of the Berkeley Historical Society. *Looking Back at Berkeley: A Pictorial History of a Diverse City*. Berkeley. Berkeley Historical Society, 1984.

Bernhardi, Robert. *The Buildings of Berkeley*. Oakland. Berkeley Architectural Heritage Association and Forest Hill Press, 1984.

Cerny, Susan Binkelspiel. *Berkeley Landmarks: An Illustrated Guide to Berkeley*. California's Architectural Heritage. Berkeley. Berkeley Architectural Heritage Association, 2001.

Drury, Wells (Ed.). *A Journal of a City's Progress*. Berkeley. Berkeley Chamber of Commerce, 1911.

Ferrier, William Warren. *Berkeley California: the Story of the Evolution of a Hamlet into a City of Culture and Commerce*. Berkeley. Sather Gate Bookstore, 1933.

41 Walking Tours of Berkeley, Cal. Revised Edition. Berkeley. Berkeley Architectural Heritage Association, 2000.

Gates, Barbara. *Already Home: A Topography of Spirit and Place*. Boston. Shambala, 2003.

Helfand, Harvey. *University of California, Berkeley: the Campus Guide*. New York. Princeton Architectural Press, 2002.

Margolin, Malcolm. *The Ohlone Way: Indian Life in the San Francisco-Monterey Bay Area*. Berkeley. Heyday Books, 1978.

McArdle, Phil (Ed.). *Exactly Opposite the Golden Gate: Essays on Berkeley's History 1845-1945*. Berkeley. The Berkeley Historical Society, 1986.

Northbrae. Berkeley. Berkeley Architectural Heritage Association, 1994.

Pettitt, George. *Berkeley: the Town and Gown of It*. Berkeley. Howell-North Books, 1973.

Pettitt, Kenneth. *Berkeley AnteBellum*. Berkeley. Kenneth Pettitt, 1995.

Pitcher, Don. *Berkeley Inside/Out: A Guide to Restaurants, Entertainment, People and Politics*. Berkeley. Heyday Books, 1989.

Willes, Burlington (Ed.). *Picturing Berkeley: A Postcard History*. Berkeley. Berkeley Architectural Heritage Association and The Berkeley Historical Society, 2002.

Willes, Burlington. *Tales from the Elmwood: A Community Memory*. Berkeley Historical Society, 2000.

Wollenberg, Charles. *Berkeley, A City in History*. http://berkeleypubliclibrary.org/system/historytext.html. Berkeley Public Library, 2002.

Works Progress Administration Writers Program. *Berkeley: The First Seventy-Five Years*. Berkeley. Gillick Press, 1941.

Acknowledgments

For over four decades Steve Manning has been a fellow traveler in the study of photography and natural history. A remarkable polymath, he has always graciously shared his knowledge. Sayre Van Young of the library's Berkeley History Room generously supported the project. The publications and resources of the Berkeley Historical Society and Berkeley Architectural Society are gratefully appreciated. John Soloman of Caffe Venezia guided us through the How Berkeley Can You Be? parade. Lynn Yarris and Paul Preuss of Lawrence Berkeley Lab explained the science behind the photographs. Amy Thomas of Pegasus and Pendragon Books; Nicholas Setka of Black Oak Books; Malcolm Margolin, David Isaacson and Lisa Manwill of Heyday Books; Kate Lydon of Saturate Design; Lindy Hough, Richard Grossinger and Minda Armstrong of North Atlantic Books; and Lynne Withey and Anthony Crouch of the University of California Press kindly shared their knowledge of the book trade. A complete review of the photographs by Christina Seely created new concepts and visions. Verónica Moscoso, Joann Sullivan and Margaret Sullivan supported the research effort. Contee Seely, Daphne O'Neal and John Selawsky proofread the text. Nick Sullivan assisted in the mechanics of photography and Photoshop. Many others freely gave their knowledge and support.

All the photographs were taken by Jon Sullivan, except those on pages 24, 26-top, 52, 53-bottom and 121, which were taken by Christina Seely, and the small photograph on page 101, which was supplied by the artist. The dust jacket photograph of Jon is by Contee Seely. Design and layout are by Jon Sullivan and Contee Seely. Jon Sullivan did all the writing except where otherwise noted.

Notes on Method

Most of the photographs were taken with a Nikon N80 using a Nikkor 28-70mm f/2.8 lens and a Nikkor 80-200mm f/2.8mm lens. The photo on page 13 was taken with a Nikon D70s. The covers and Berkeley at night were done with a Mamiya RZ67 with a 50mm lens. Generally Kodak Professional Portra 160-VC, 400-VC and 800 color print films were used. A Microtek ScanMaker 8700 converted the 35mm film to digital format. The images were prepared for publication in Photoshop and QuarkXPress. Digital manipulation was kept within the confines of a traditional darkroom except in a few cases. The sky was colored on page 24 and the right photograph on page 147. Hair was slightly rearranged on page 75. Graffiti was removed from the left photograph on page 116. A sun flare was removed from the image on page 144. Working images were printed on an Epson 2000P.

Ordering Photographs

Photographs can be ordered from http://www.berkeleyoneandonly.com. Most images can be ordered on matte or glossy paper in sizes 5 x 7 and 8 x 10 or in the same size as appears here. Photographs are printed on an Epson 2000P or equivalent with Epson archival ink.

Early residents saw the Golden Gate as symbolic of the passage to the hereafter and were offended by the construction of the bridge. In mid-February the sun sets in the center of the channel.

Night envelops Berkeley. A strip of white light
reaching toward the bay traces University Avenue.
The towers of the Golden Gate Bridge are marked
by points of red light.